JACK BOTERMANS

HIGH-FLYING
PAPER
AIRPLANES

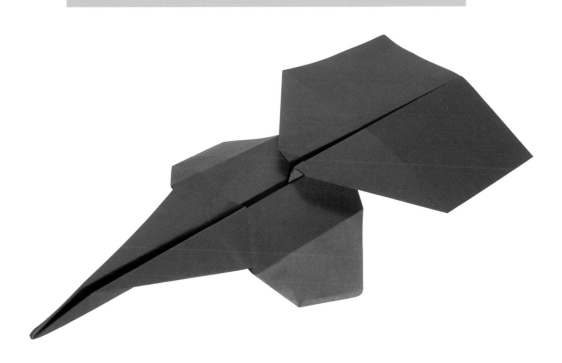

Sterling Publishing Co., Inc.
New York

Translated from the Dutch by Carla van Splunteren, Canada/Netherlands

Library of Congress Cataloging-in-Publication Data Available

10 9 8 7 6 5 4 3 2 1

Published by Sterling Publishing Co., Inc.
387 Park Avenue South, New York, NY 10016
© 2004 Bookman International by Jack Botermans, Netherlands
Originally published in the Dutch language under the title *Vliegen met Papier 2*.
Concept, text, models, photography, illustrations and design by Jack Botermans,
Netherlands
Edited by Heleen Tichler, Netherlands
English translation copyright © 2005 by Sterling Publishing Co., Inc.

Distributed in Canada by Sterling Publishing
c/o Canadian Manda Group, 165 Dufferin Street
Toronto, Ontario, Canada M6K 3H6
Distributed in Great Britain and Europe by Chris Lloyd at Orca Book
Services, Stanley House, Fleets Lane, Poole BH15 3AJ, England
Distributed in Australia by Capricorn Link (Australia) Pty. Ltd.
P.O. Box 704, Windsor, NSW 2756, Australia

Printed in China

Sterling ISBN: 1-4027-1725-3 Hardcover
         ISBN: 1-4027-2422-5 Paperback
For information about custom editions, special sales, premium
and corporate purchases, please contact Sterling Special Sales
Department at 800-805-5489 or specialsales@sterlingpub.com.

One bird in the air is worth two on the ground...

CONTENTS

A maiden flight can be organized in many different ways.

People cannot fly. That's an indisputable fact. They don't have wings, do they? But that hasn't kept them from striving to be able to glide through the air. And to do just that, humans invented the airplane.

The first person who dreamed about this wasn't taken seriously at all: Leonardo da Vinci was simply ridiculed. But the dreamers were inventive and persistent, and in 1903 they proved themselves right when the first official flight with a flying machine was made. Thereafter things went quickly in the world of aviation, and nowadays we don't think twice about boarding a plane to get to a given destination.

But people will always remain dreamers. Air trips to destinations far away are practical, impressive if you will, but you can't play with real airplanes or make them yourself. And thus people started using their imagination and inventiveness again. They started imitating reality—this time not with aluminum or high-quality plastics, but merely with paper. A couple of folds in a sheet, a strong sweep of the arm, and off it glides. Flying with paper requires well-thought-out models that have the same qualities real airplanes have. They must not only look good, but also be able to make long glides, good loops or barrel rolls, and other stunts.

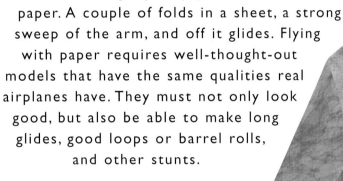

The Wing-Nose in a dive—a good example of experimental folding and flying.

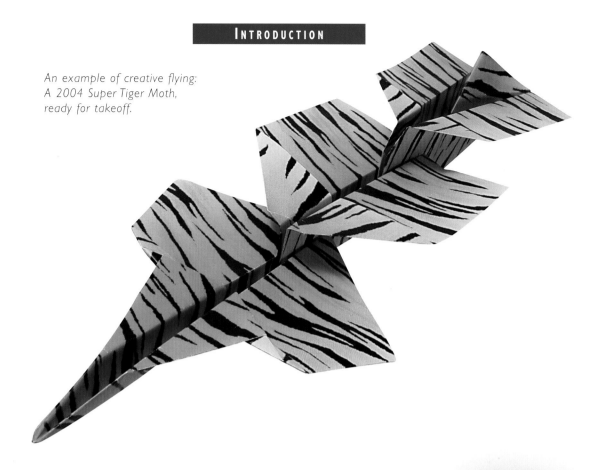

An example of creative flying:
A 2004 Super Tiger Moth,
ready for takeoff.

As entertainment you can, of course, organize a pickle-spitting or ice-cube-sitting contest. Either would certainly let you see your friends and colleagues in a different light, but why make all the effort when it could be so much easier? After all, there's always plenty of paper available in every office. That's all you need for a good paper airplane flying contest.

The Japanese art of paper folding, origami, is a good basis for making terrific airplanes. With the help of the basic origami techniques, you can go a long way. We compiled this book after the success of our first one, *Flying with Paper*, in order to elaborate on the fascinating world of flying with paper airplanes. Using origami techniques, we illustrate many new models in this book. Categorized in the chapters "Distance Crackers," "Experimental Models," "Stunt Flyers," and "Creative Flights," we hope to give the readers a lot of ideas on how you can to build awesome airplanes in a simple way. The chapter "Creative Flights" especially stands out in the making of extraordinary models and gives an extra insight into building paper airplanes.

So. . . . ready for takeoff?

Your hands are the most important piece of equipment for folding paper airplanes. Some models need more, but even then a few simple items will suffice. When folding airplanes, work precisely and study the drawings well before starting; if you don't understand something at first, look carefully, study the next drawing, and everything will become evident. Patience pays off!

GENERAL

Work on a clean surface and keep everything neat and organized. The weight of the paper needed for folding an airplane correlates with the size of the model. For the models between 4 and 8 inches, 60-gram paper is necessary. The models we use in this book are mainly based on 80-gram paper. Complicated folding patterns require thin paper, even as thin as tissue paper, but those are for experienced folders. One rule applies at all times: the bigger the model, the heavier the paper. But you can always experiment; sometimes the qualities improve with lighter paper. If you don't know exactly what kind of 80-gram paper you should use, start with a piece of printer or copy paper.

Always study the drawings before you start folding, so you can see what the result should look like. Look closely at the picture of the model. Sometimes a picture is worth a thousand words. To get folds to be nice and sharp, you can make grooves in the paper prior to folding by drawing the sharp point of a pair of scissors firmly against a ruler along the line where the fold will be. You can also semi-slice the paper with a knife where the fold will be, but only do this with heavier paper and be careful not to cut through the paper. Some patterns require a double fold. This means that you fold the paper to both sides, so resulting in a supple hinge fold.

EXPLANATION OF ILLUSTRATIONS

Dotted line: the place to make the fold. *Thin solid line:* the place where a previous fold has been made. *Scissors:* cut as shown. *Arrow:* in the direction of the fold. (An oval-shaped arrow indicates that the model must be turned over.) *A fold going in the opposite direction:* first fold it back and forth on the dotted line, and then fold the upper point to the inside as shown by the arrow. The *zigzag arrow* indicates that first a fold must be made to the inside, and then one to the outside. Follow the direction of the arrow precisely to ensure that nothing goes wrong.

EQUIPMENT

You need only a few items: a small, sharp pair of scissors (preferably hairdresser's scissors), an HB or B pencil to mark distances, (make sure the lead is not too hard, so it's easy to erase), a hobby knife with a retractable blade that can be broken off if it gets dull, a stapler, tape, and good paper glue to glue surfaces together when necessary. Finally, you'll need a ruler to make straight folds and to make the paper the right size. Good luck folding!

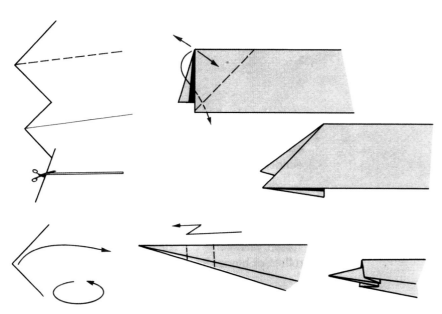

This type will amaze you by the vast distances it can cover.

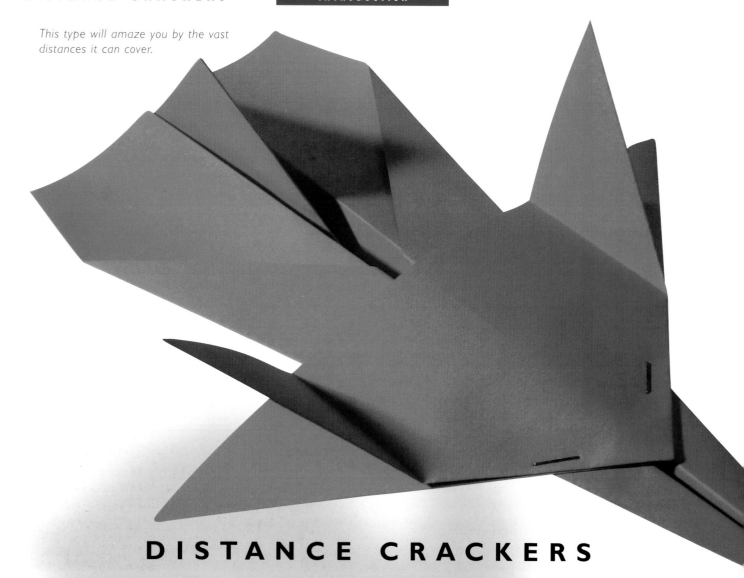

DISTANCE CRACKERS

Most paper airplanes are quickly folded. But the question remains as to whether they can fly fast and far. In many contests for paper airplane makers, it's about the distance the design can cover, thrown from a standing position. Distances of 150 feet (45 m) and more have been achieved. In the next chapter we will show you a few models that have been designed especially to cover vast distances. You can make great models with simple printer or copy paper and refined folding techniques. Once you've made your first model, you have to break it in, adjusting the wing tips to give a long, and straight flight. Don't give up too soon; you may have to fold several samples of the same model before you eventually find the right balance.

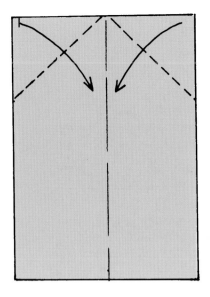

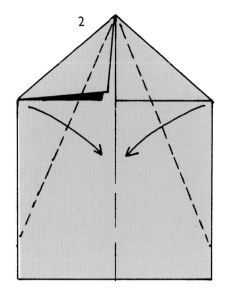

2

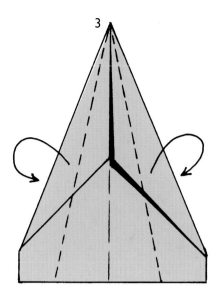

3

THE BODY

Everybody has folded the body of a paper airplane at least once. This one is fast and easy to make, and the whole thing is folded from two sheets of 8½ x 11 inch paper. The rudders can be folded so as to influence the flying pattern, as shown.

1. Fold a sheet of 8½ x 11 inch paper in half lengthwise and reopen it. Then bring the two corners to the middle fold, folding on the dotted line.

2. Fold the two sides on the dotted lines to the middle fold.

3. Repeat this with the two sides but then fold them to the back.

4. Fold the model in half along the dotted line.

4

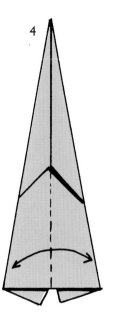

5

5. Staple the wings together at the arrow after having pulled them down a little. Fold the back on the dotted line toward the inside and upward to make a stabilizer (See page 7; the wing will be described on the next page).

This is the body of the Long-Distance Glider. This flies superbly as is and is well suited to serve as a basis for other models.

1

2

3

4

THE WING

1. Take the second sheet of paper and fold an upper corner onto the opposite side. Cut the excess strip of paper off to make a square.

2. Fold the (now square) piece of paper from both diagonals back and forth. Do the same at the fold in the middle.

3. Fold the sheet in half, pushing the sides into the middle.

4. Flatten it well. Fold the top corner points upward and form the stabilizers on the wing. Staple it together at the body (See drawing).

FLYING INSTRUCTIONS

Use heavy paper for this airplane. It is especially suited for flying vast distances. Hold the plane under the nose and throw with great force. By bending the backside of the body slightly upward, the distance the plane flies will increase.

If you position the wing tips at less than 45 degrees, it will lengthen flight time. It will, however, not fly as straight.

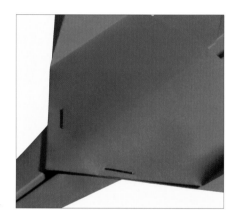

The wing of the Long-Distance Glider. With two staples securing it to the body, it gives the airplane tremendous lift, through which great distances can be achieved.

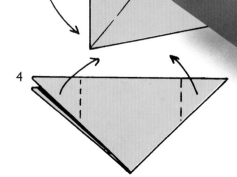

The name says it all. These airplanes are easy to fold, so you can make a whole fleet in different colors and let them circle down together from the top of the stairs.

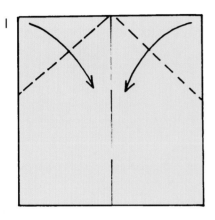

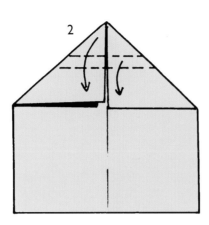

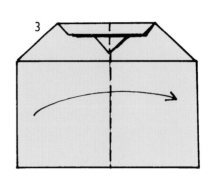

1. Fold the two opposite corners of a square sheet of 8½ x 11 inch paper toward each other.

2. Fold the point downward to the middle of the triangle. Then fold a ½-inch edge over that.

3. Fold the figure in half at the dotted line in the middle.

4. Fold the flaps to the outside. Staple the nose. Cut the wings at point *a*.

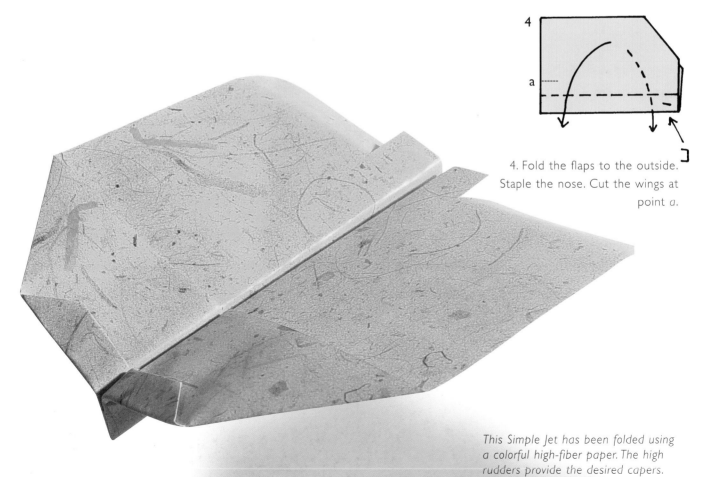

This Simple Jet has been folded using a colorful high-fiber paper. The high rudders provide the desired capers.

11

SUPER JET COUGAR

This airplane is the prototype of the speed devil, just like the cougar. In the air the Super Jet Cougar has still more good qualities: stability and stamina. Not suitable for acrobatic stunts, but a superb glider.

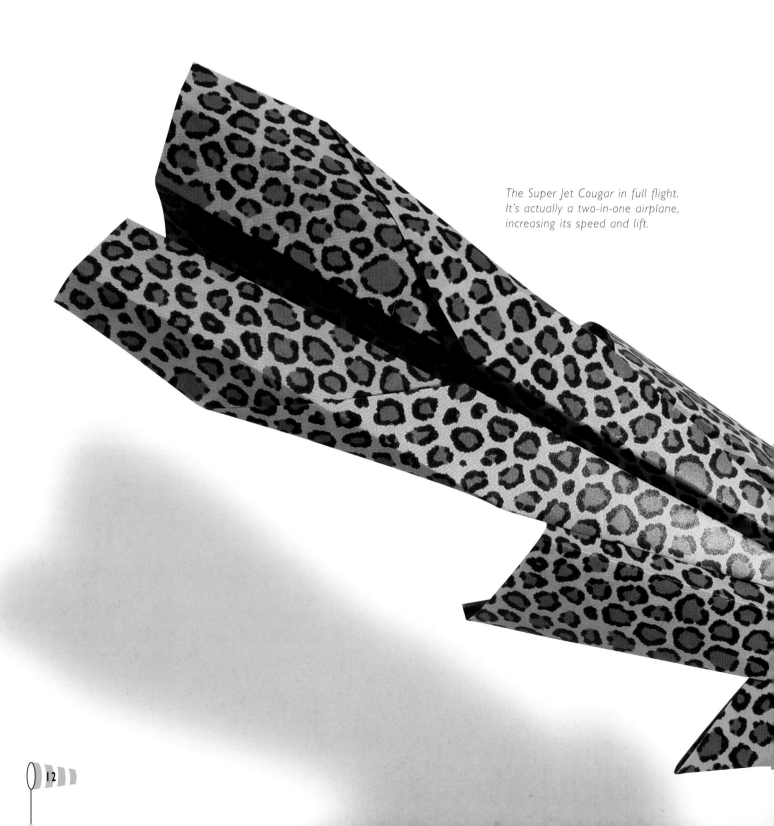

The Super Jet Cougar in full flight. It's actually a two-in-one airplane, increasing its speed and lift.

I

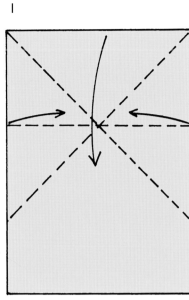

THE NOSE

1. Fold a sheet of 8½ x 11 inch paper on the diagonals of the uppermost square back and forth, and then horizontally on the corner of the diagonals.

2. Fold the top back and at the same time fold two sides to the inside. Now fold the two lower side flaps toward the inside.

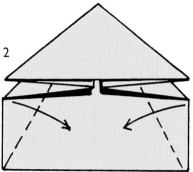

2

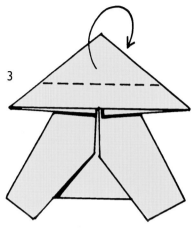

3

3. Fold the point to the back.

5. Fold the point upward and subsequently the whole model in half.

6. The final fold is the upper half towards the outside on both sides. The nose is finished.

4. Turn the whole thing over.

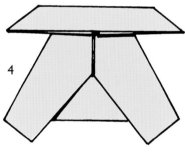

4

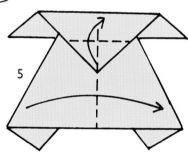

5

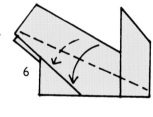

6

This is what the nose looks like when it's done. It's a nice airplane, even though its wings are a little narrow.

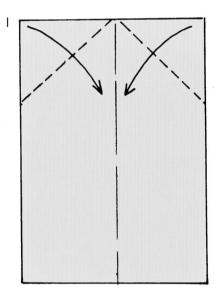

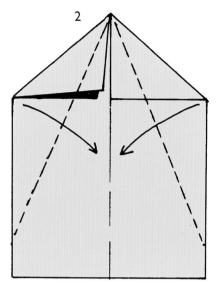

THE TAIL

1. Fold the upper corners of an 8½ x 11 inch sheet to the middle line.

2. Fold the sides to the middle.

3. Fold the whole thing in half.

4. Fold both sides twice to the outside. Put the whole model in the nose and staple it securely.

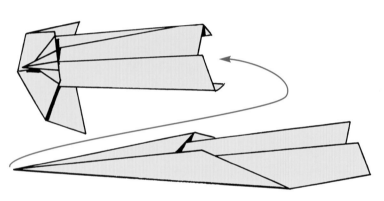

This is how the tail is supposed to look. It is pushed into the nose and secured with a staple. The tail can function as an airplane on its own.

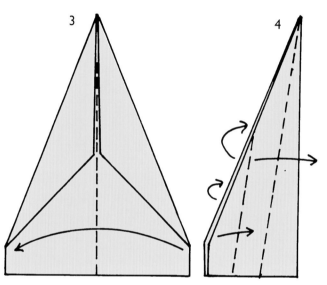

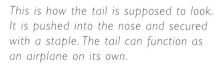

You'll have this plane made before you can count to ten. And does it ever fly! Simple and straightforward, yet a great distance cracker, it is very easy to trim with the rear wing points. This is the ideal airplane with which to organize distance flight contests.

A square airplane built before you can count to ten? What more could you want? Should it crash you can make another one in a jiffy.

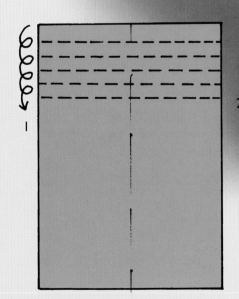

1. Fold an 8½ x 11 inch sheet five times on the short side.

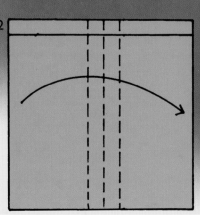

2. and 3. Fold the whole thing in half and make the wings by folding them to either side. Secure the nose with a staple.

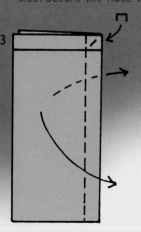

A fast-flying model that, if well trimmed, is suitable for trick flying. According to a Chinese proverb, airplanes without wings cannot fly, but wings without airplanes can. Wings provide the lift for the body, but you can of course eliminate the body. That is actually the case with the Arrowhead, and it gives it a vast flight range. In addition, this model can be used as the basis for your own fantasy creations.

The Arrowhead, a fine airplane with good flying qualities. The wings lend themselves to decoration with personal insignia.

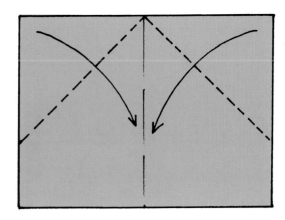

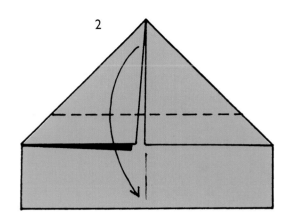

1. Fold an 8½ x 11 inch sheet across the width in the middle. Reopen the sheet. Fold the two upper corners against the middle.

2. Fold the point downward even with the bottom of the sheet.

3. Now comes the hard part. Fold the points *a* to the inside, pulling points *b* downward. This will make folds on the dotted lines.

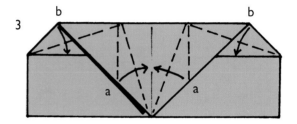

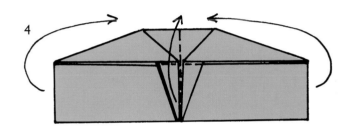

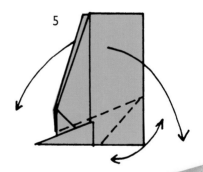

4. Fold the point upward and fold the model in half toward the back.

5. Make a fold in the tail back and forth. Crease the fold by pressing down hard. Next, fold the back point toward the inside and upward to make a tail rudder. Unfold the wings on the dotted line. The Arrowhead is ready for takeoff.

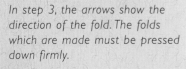

In step 3, the arrows show the direction of the fold. The folds which are made must be pressed down firmly.

The SU-27 was developed during the 1970s as a direct answer to the U.S. Air Force's McDonnell Douglas F-15 fighter. The SU-27's plane's performance was outstanding, like that of this paper model. This plane is extremely well suited to hit a target from a distance.

The Sukhoi SU-27, a fast and effective airplane.

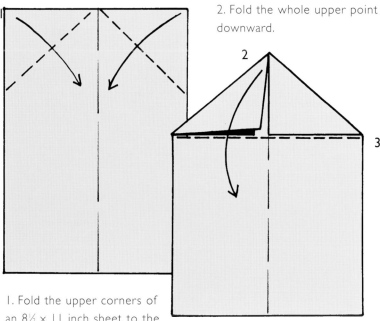

2. Fold the whole upper point downward.

3. Then fold the point on the dotted line back upward again.

1. Fold the upper corners of an 8½ x 11 inch sheet to the middle.

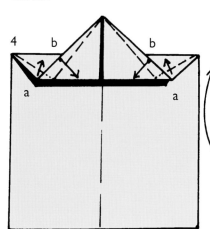

4. These folds require precise attention. Fold the points a upward and the points b downward. This will create the folds as shown. Press firmly. Look at the drawing and photo for the result.

5. Fold the whole model in half, backward.

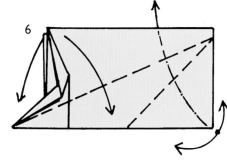

6. Make a stabilizer by folding the back points back and forth and then toward the inside and upward. Next you fold the wings on the upper dotted line upward.

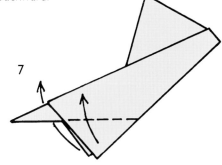

7. Now you only have to fold the wing tips upward.

This photograph shows the plane after step 4.

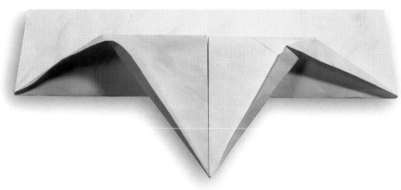

Why not make a whole herd of flying cows? Not fast but steady, the Flying Cow is the ideal airplane to fold in great numbers.

The Flying Cow has real long-distance qualities. Not fast but steady, like a cow grazing. The lift of the wings is great and keeps it in the air for a long time. You must spend quite some time trimming the wings, in order to get it to do what you want. The Flying Cow is very suitable for use as a stunt airplane. Should you wish to make it more stable, insert a long, narrow double-folded piece of paper in the rear part.

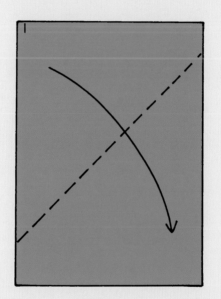

1. Fold an 8½ × 11 inch sheet at a slant on the dotted line. Press firmly.

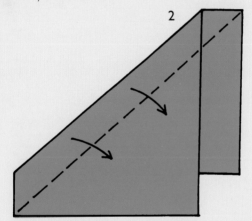

2. Fold the edge on the long slanted side approximately ¾ inch.

3. Fold the whole model on the dotted line in half. Press this fold firmly as well.

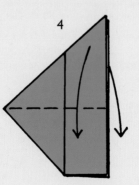

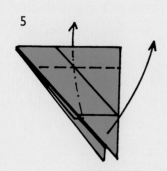

4. Turn the model, so that it is facing you as shown in the drawing. Fold the wings down, one to each side. Fold them in half and press the fold firmly.

5. Now determine the position of the wings by folding the two lower points 90 degrees upward. A staple or some glue in the nose will keeps the whole model together for the first trial flight.

By adding a horizontal airscrew to an airplane, you increase the lift through the resistance of the air during a descending flight. We did that here with the Heli-Plane, a combination of two independent airplanes. The airscrew itself functions as an airplane; the body does the same. Together they beat it all. Vast distances can be covered with it. You shouldn't throw the Heli-Plane too hard, rather, let it glide slowly through the air.

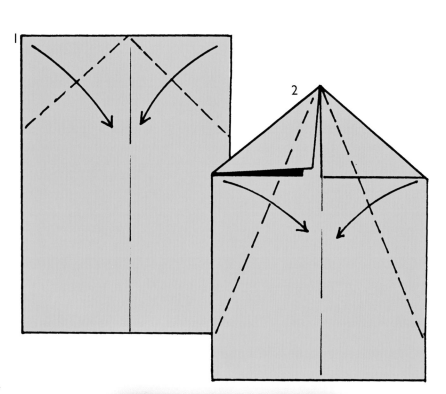

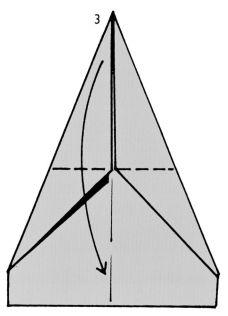

THE BODY

1. Fold an 8½ x 11 inch sheet in half and reopen it. Fold the upper corners toward the middle.

2. Fold the sides again against the middle line.

3. Fold the uppermost point exactly onto the bottom.

The photograph opposite shows the plane after step 3.

The Heli-Plane is an obvious
combination of two independent
airplanes. The airscrew and body can
function separately from each other.

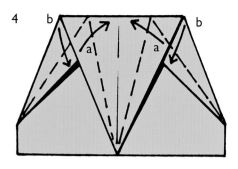

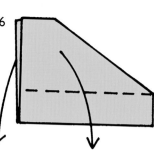

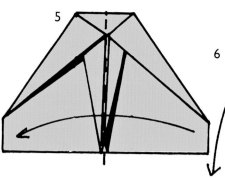

4. Fold the points *a* upward, resulting in points *b* being folded under. Study the photograph of the previous page closely.

5. After pressing the whole model firmly, fold it in half.

6. Fold the wings on the dotted line toward the outside. Fasten the front of the nose with a staple. Then fold the neck for the airscrew back and forth on a diagonal. After this bring it upward through the middle.

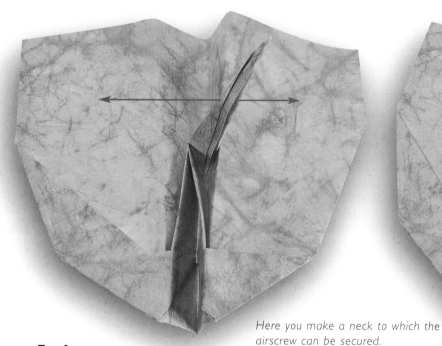

Here you make a neck to which the airscrew can be secured.

THE AIRSCREW

For the airscrew do the following:
1. Take a 4 × 8 inch sheet of paper. Fold the two opposite corners in half.

2. Fold the whole thing in half on the dotted line and fold it open.

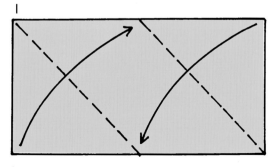

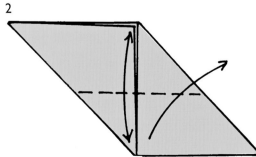

3

The airscrew after step 4.

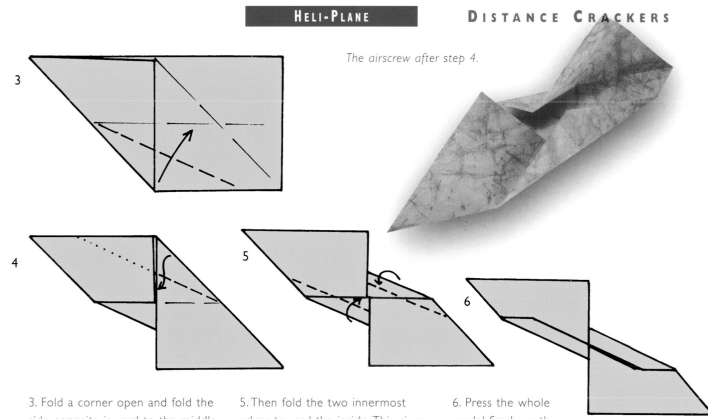

4

5

6

3. Fold a corner open and fold the side opposite inward to the middle. Then you fold the big flap back again.

4. Do the same thing with the opposite side. Open the big flap first. Fold the side opposite inward on the dotted line and the flap back again.

5. Then fold the two innermost edges toward the inside. This gives the airscrew lengthwise support.

6. Press the whole model firmly so the folds are flat. Secure the airscrew onto the neck with a pin.

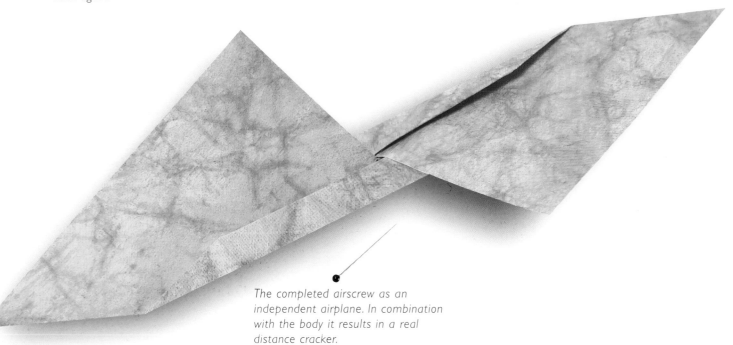

The completed airscrew as an independent airplane. In combination with the body it results in a real distance cracker.

In August 1931 Pan American Airways published a specifications for a new type of flying boat. There was a need for this type of boat for the transatlantic service that the company wished to begin. They wanted an aircraft with an enormous (in those days) range—2,500 miles (4023 km). Our version is smaller-scaled but has an impressive range. This Sikorsky is made up of two pieces, each of which has good flying qualities. Joined together, they form the ultimate distance cracker. (By the way, landing on water is not an option for this paper model.)

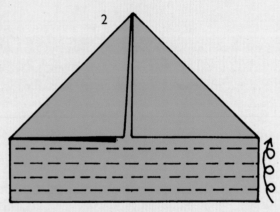

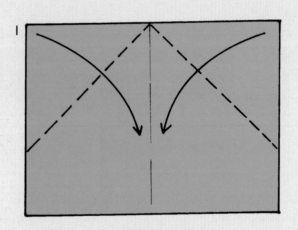

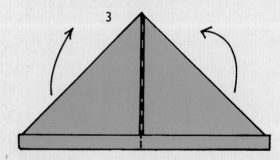

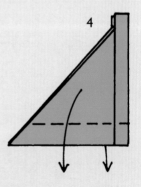

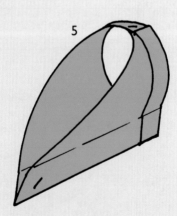

THE NOSE

1. Take an 8½ x 11 inch sheet of paper. Fold it exactly in the middle across the width. Fold both upper corners to the inside against the fold.

2. Fold the lower flap in strips approximately 1 inch upward and press them firmly until they've flattened.

3. Fold the whole model in half.

4. Fold the nose wings on the dotted line to the outside.

5. Staple the front of the nose. Staple the wings together at the tips. Shape the model until it has a cylindrical shape.

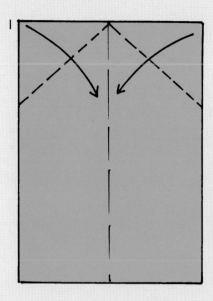

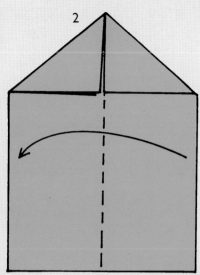

2. Fold the whole model in half.

3. Make the tail wings by folding these toward the outside on the dotted line.

4. Slide nose and tailpiece into each other and staple together.

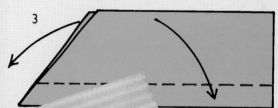

THE TAIL

1. Fold a 8½ x 11 inch sheet of paper in the middle, lengthwise. Fold both upper corners towards the inside, to the fold.

The Sikorsky S-42 in full flight.

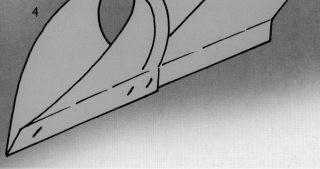

A wing with lift and a body with potential for gliding flight—these are the characteristics of the Double-Wing Special in a nutshell. The wing is actually a variation on the standard manner of folding already demonstrated. You can modify the flying qualities of this model not only by adding an aileron, but also by combining the basic properties of other models in this book.

A wing with lift and a body with potential for gliding flights—the characteristics of the Double-Wing Special.

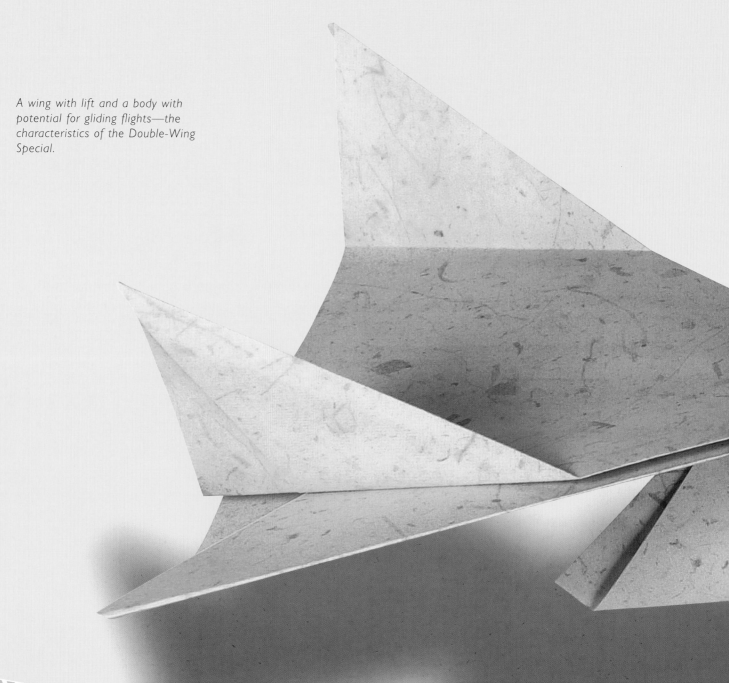

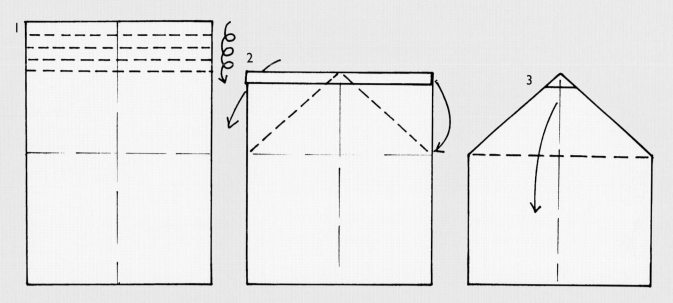

THE NOSE

1. Take an 8½ x 11 inch sheet of paper and make a fold in the middle across the length and width. Make a sturdy edge on the dotted line on the top by folding the paper five times.

2. Fold the upper corners toward the back, but in such a way that the undersides of the corners come out exactly in the middle of the sheet.

3. Now fold the point towards you and press the fold firmly.

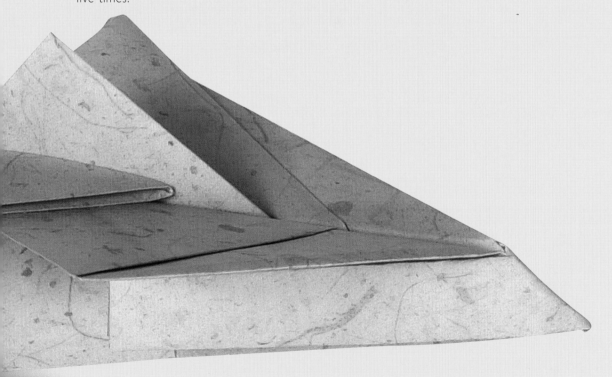

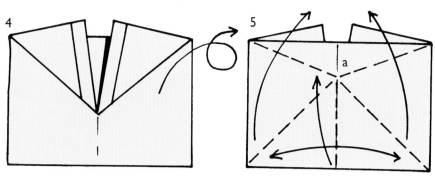

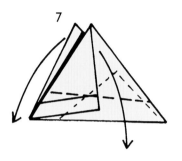

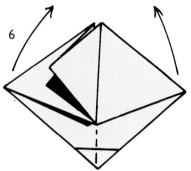

4. As you can see in the drawing, only the points must be folded, not the flaps underneath them. These now stick out on a slant facing upward.

5. Now it gets complicated. Take the point underneath and bring it upward, keeping your finger on point a. In this way the folds will appear, as shown by the dotted lines. It is actually four folds at once. Look at the picture carefully and don't give up too soon. You can make the folds one at a time and then pull them all up at once.

6. Fold the whole model in half.

7. Now make the nose wings by folding them to the side.

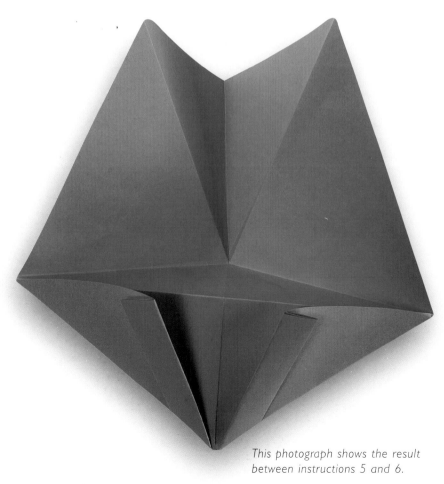

This photograph shows the result between instructions 5 and 6.

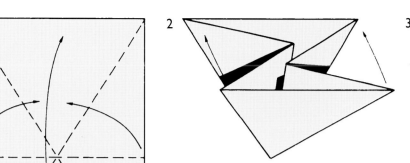 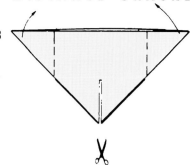

THE WING

1. Fold an 8½ x 11 inch sheet diagonally in the middle of the cross points of the diagonals. It is advisable to fold all the folds to both sides.

2. Press the sides at the indicated points, which will fall next to each other because of the rectangular form, making this figure.

3. Fold the upper layer of the wing tips on the dotted line in a square corner upward and make a cut as indicated. Glue the front edges of the wings to each other. Staple the nose and the wing together on both sides of the front stabilizer.

The Double-Wing Special folded using different colors of paper. The wings have been secured with staples. Not very attractive, but sturdy.

The Fairey FD.2 comes flashing by.
This supersonic model works well when
made with paper.

After several experiments in 1947 with vertically launched models where the viability of the delta wing was apparent, Fairey was asked to research the possibilities of supersonic models with delta wings. That's how this model, which established a new speed record of 1,132 mph (1822 kph) in March 1956, was created. Inspired by the FD.2, we designed this paper model. It won't fly 1,132 mph (1822 kph), but it is an excellent flyer for great distances.

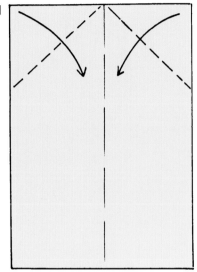

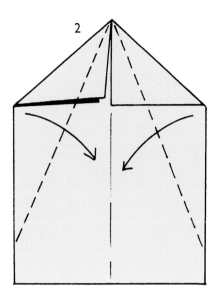

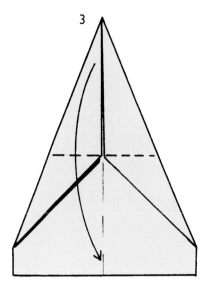

THE BODY WITH WINGS

1. Take an 8½ x 11 inch sheet of paper and make a fold in the middle lengthwise. Fold the two upper corners to the middle.

2. Next, fold both sides on the dotted line to the middle fold.

3. Fold the point downward to the underside of the paper.

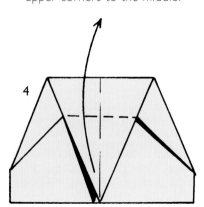

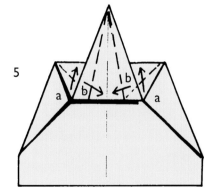

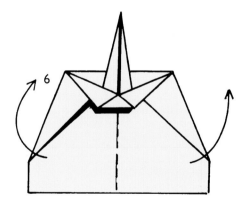

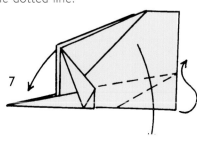

4. Then fold the point upward on the dotted line.

5. Fold the points *a* upward while at the same time folding points *b* toward the inside. This will make folds on the dotted lines. Press the whole thing flat.

6. Fold the whole model toward the back.

7. Make a fold under the tail and push it to the inside and up, making a stabilizer. Fold the wings on the dotted line on both sides toward the outside. Now it's time for the tail.

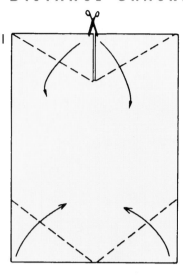

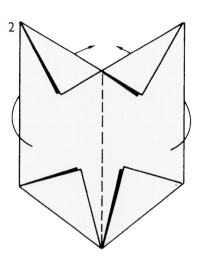

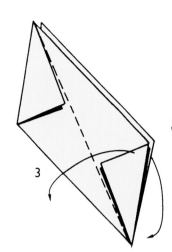

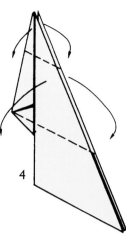

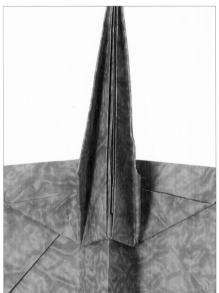

The tail is placed on the stabilizer as shown. The whole thing is held together with a staple. Be sure that the wing tails have exactly the same position as the body wings.

THE TAIL

1. Cut an 8½ x 11 inch sheet in the middle from the top inward and fold the flaps on the dotted line downward. Fold the flap underneath upward, as shown.

2. Fold the whole model in half toward the back.

3. Now fold both sides on the diagonal dotted line toward the outside.

4. Fold the upper points on the dotted line toward the outside. Then form the stabilizer surface by folding the tail on the dotted line under it. Glue the two bottom halves to each other.

5. Slide the base into the tail and glue. The FD.2 is ready for its maiden flight.

This is how the stabilizer is placed on the body, then attached to it with a staple. Make sure that the tail wings are in exactly the same position as the body wings.

EXPERIMENTAL MODELS

Until now the folding has been fairly straightforward. There are, however, many more possibilities in the field of paper airplanes. The greatest advantage of paper is that you can experiment as much as you want. It costs millions to develop a real airplane and many years to achieve a prototype, whereas with paper you're done a lot sooner. And on the experimental side, you can indulge yourself quite a lot more.

Does your airplane practically fly into the wastepaper basket all by itself? No problem—you can make an improved version in a jiffy. You can use different sorts of paper to discover what works the best, or make small changes to improve the performance of your airplane. Especially with these airplanes you can easily leave the familiar behind. Who knows what a revolutionary discovery you'll make!

The Concorde, created by France's Sud Aviation and the British Aircraft Corporation, has shown us through the years that it is one of the better jet airplanes. The delta-wing concept, which was quickly abandoned by many airplane builders, was implemented with great success in the Concorde. This wing, together with the well-known pointed nose, gives the Concorde its characteristic appearance. The paper version of the Concorde has the same qualities as the original—it skims through the air like an arrow and is just as recognizable. Only the price difference is striking: this item costs a few cents, and the real one costs many, many millions.

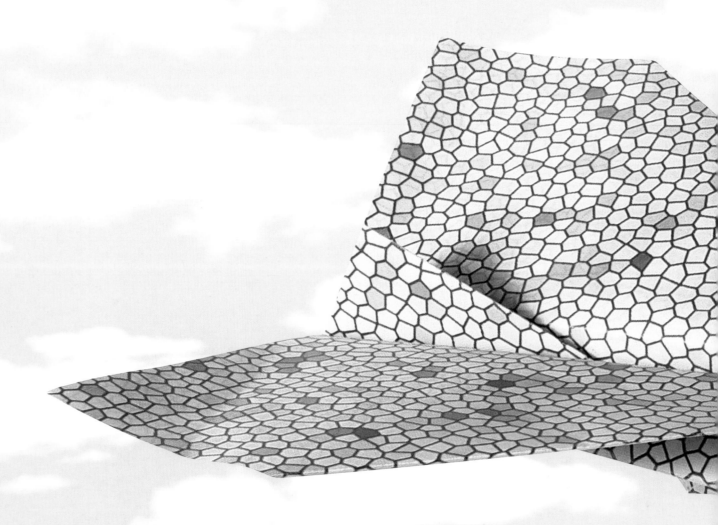

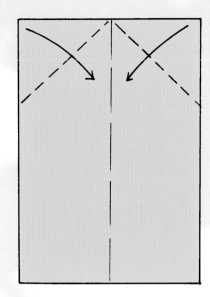
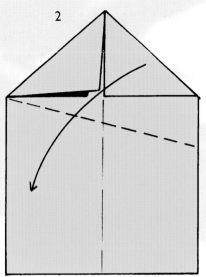
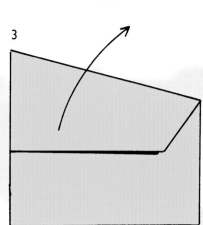

1. Take an 8½ x 11 inch sheet of paper and make a fold in the middle, lengthwise. Next, fold the upper corners to this fold.

2. and 3. Fold the slanted right top side downward along the long side and back up again.

The Concorde in low pass. The plane makes a wonderful paper experiment—not easy to fold, but an airplane with a fantastic flying capacity.

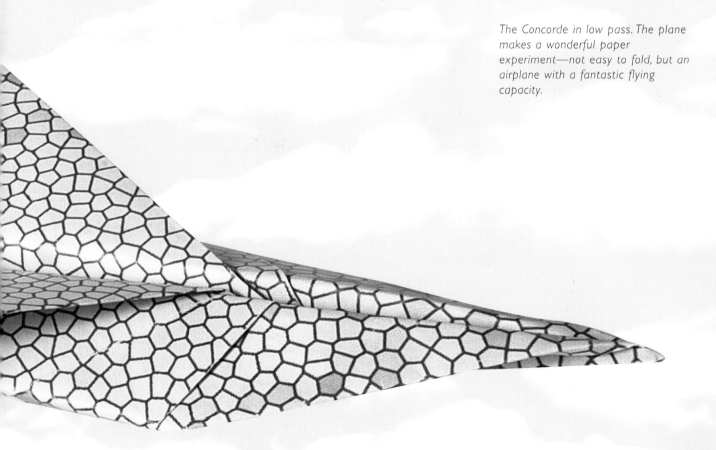

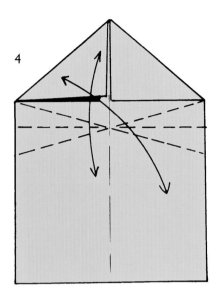

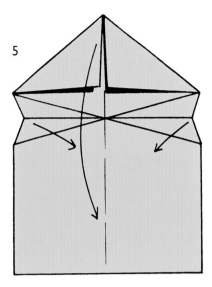

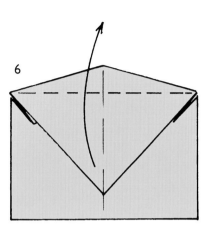

4. Repeat the previous two steps with the left side as well. Then fold the point downward on the dotted line. Make these folds double (backward and forward) to make the next step easier.

5. Fold the upper point downward and at the same time fold the two sides toward the inside. The two sides will come between the point and the sheet on the back side.

6. Fold the point upward again, on the dotted line. Press all the folds flat.

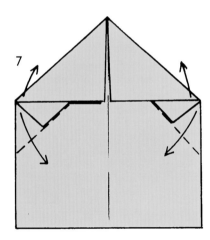

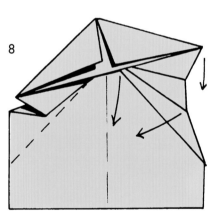

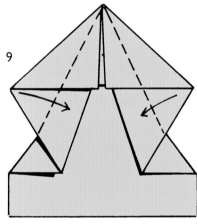

7. This step is a difficult one. Pull the top layer on the two corners on the sides upward. Then fold the underlying flaps on the dotted line toward the inside.

8. By pulling the bottom of the triangle up a little it's possible to fold the side points of the underlying flaps toward the inside.

9. Fold the sides on the dotted line toward the inside. Flatten all the folds well by pressing.

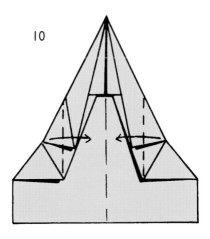

10

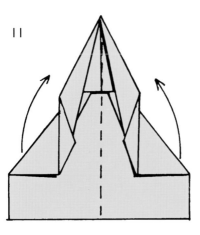

11

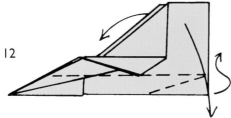

12

10. Fold the side points as shown in the drawing toward the inside. These will form the jet motors later on.

11. Fold the whole model in half toward the back.

12. Fold the tail diagonally back and forth toward the inside and upward. Fold each wing to the side.

The Concorde is an expensive airplane. This paper version is valuable too. Folded with a 500-Euro bill, it makes you proceed with caution when flying it.

Undetectable by radar, the Stealth Bomber swishes through the air. In reality it is made of carbon, but paper is perfectly satisfactory for our purposes. It has an enormous flight range, as it is actually one big wing. One advantage of a paper model is: it cannot carry bombs.

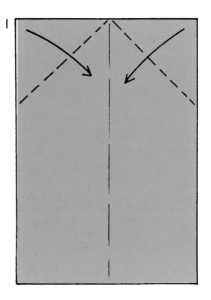

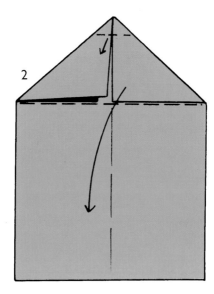

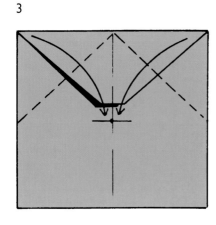

1. Take an 8½ x 11 inch sheet of paper. Fold it in the middle, lengthwise. Fold the two upper corners toward the inside to the fold.

2. Fold the upper point on the dotted line downward. Next, fold the whole triangle downward.

3. Fold the upper corners inward to the middle fold.

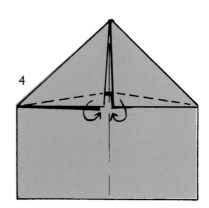

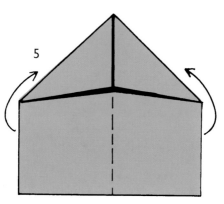

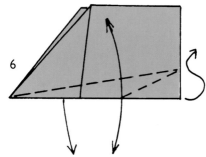

4. Fold the lowest edge of the corners you just folded inward on the dotted line. It's easiest to fold them upward first so they come exactly to the folded triangle under it. Then you fold them inward under the point with the triangle.

5. Fold the whole model in half to the back.

6. Fold the wings back and forth on the dotted line. Make a stabilizer out of the tail.

The Stealth glides silently through space. This paper model is environmentally much friendlier, as it cannot transport bombs.

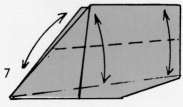

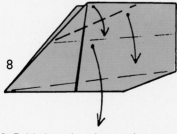

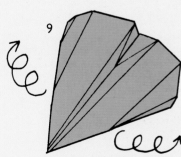

7. Fold the wings back and forth to the coinciding fold.

8. Fold the wing tips to the coinciding fold.

9. Now fold the wings into the correct position. See the model on this page. The position is very important for the flying capacity and can be adjusted as desired.

41

The Digi-Jet is a very experimental model. By folding the wings differently during the final stage you can keep making different airplanes.

Everything is digitized nowadays, including this model of paper airplane. The basis of this model has been around for decades. The way in which the nose is folded could even be called classical. It's not simple, but it's extraordinarily efficient. It requires a bit of persistence to fold this model, but the result is extremely gratifying. It's fairly simple easy to give it a personal touch during the final stages of folding. By folding the tail and wings in another direction a totally different model is created. The wing with the nose forms the basis for a good airplane that carries its weight in the front, creating good flying qualities. The tail, which in itself plays a minor role, can still exercise great influence on the flying qualities if you make it longer or shorter.

1

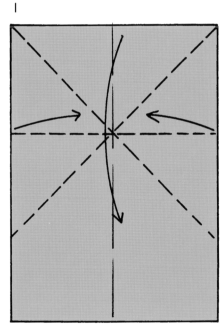

2

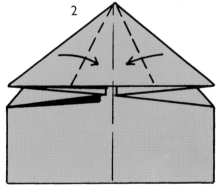

3

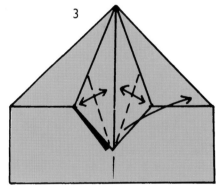

THE WING

1. Fold an 8½ x 11 inch sheet of paper over the two designated diagonals and back and forth across the width on the cross point of the diagonals. Make sure to leave an edge at the bottom. The best thing to do is first fold these in half to both sides. (You'll notice that this principle works best with most models.) Next fold the top side downward and the sides to the inside. This will create Now the model as shown above.

2. Fold the two side points toward the inside against the middle of the paper. Do this only with the points on top.

3. Make sharp folds on the two side points of the kite-shaped figure in the middle. Next, fold the right point to the outside, flat on the underlying paper.

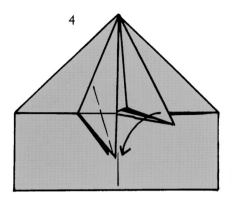

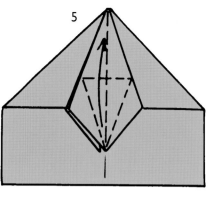

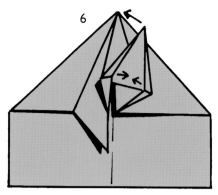

4. Here it becomes a little difficult. This step you do first with the right point and then repeat with the left one. Fold the right point open and downward. By doing this you will make the figure shown below.

5. Make crisp folds on the given dotted lines shown. Next fold the underlying point upward on the horizontal dotted line while folding the side points toward the inside at the same time.

6. As is shown in the drawing, a new, smaller kite-shaped form is made.

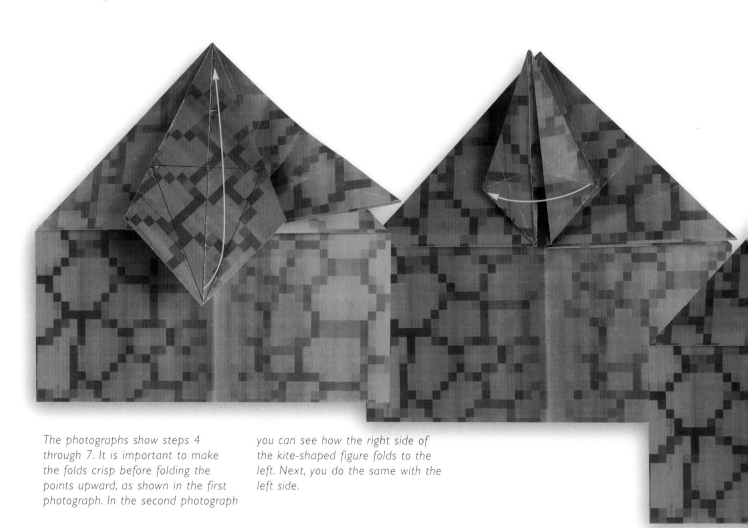

The photographs show steps 4 through 7. It is important to make the folds crisp before folding the points upward, as shown in the first photograph. In the second photograph *you can see how the right side of the kite-shaped figure folds to the left. Next, you do the same with the left side.*

This is what the nose should look like when it's completely finished. This is one of the most difficult but at the same time best noses to fold.

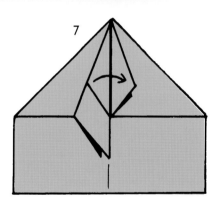

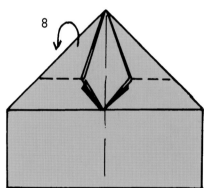

7. Fold the left half of the kite-shaped figure to the right, following the procedure in step 4. Fold the left point open and downward. In this way the figure shown on the first photograph opposite is made. Next repeat steps 5 and 6 on the left side. Finally, you fold the right half of the small kite-shaped figure to the left.

8. Fold the point to the back on the dotted line. The underlying point of the kite shape will flip up, raised from the other surface. The photograph above shows the nose and wing as it should be. Complicated, but a wing with which you can make all kinds of variations.

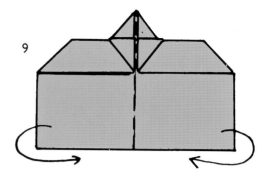

9

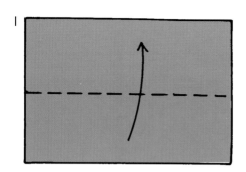

10

1

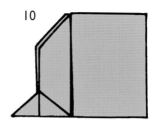

9. Fold the wing in half to the back.

10. Now fold the tail.

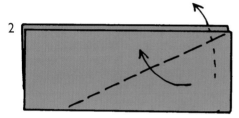

2

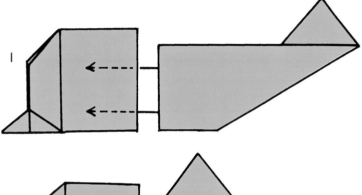

1

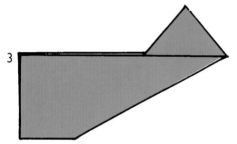

3

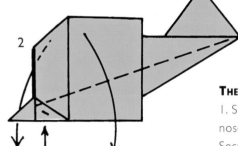

2

THE TAIL

1. Fold a 6 x 8½ inch piece of paper in half lengthwise.

2. Fold back and forth on the dotted line in order to fold the lower right point upward between the paper.

3. Now slide the tail into the nose.

THE ASSEMBLY

1. Slide the top of the tail into the nose under the designated point. Secure it with a staple.

2. Fold the wings outward on both sides on the dotted line.

The nose and the tail are separated after folding. The front of the tail goes under the point of the nose that sticks out behind.

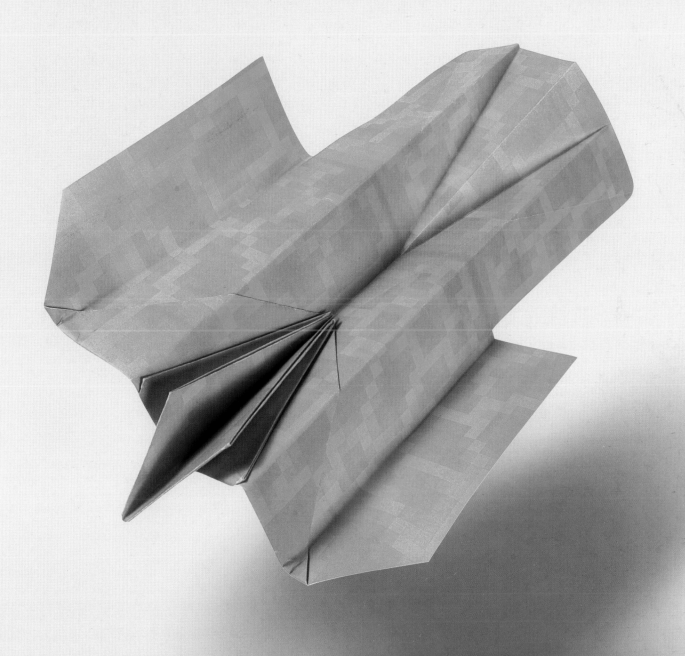

The Digi-Jet with the wings and tail folded in a different way. The result is a totally different airplane. Folded like this, the Digi-Jet is an excellent glider.

After the Korean War the Americans wanted a jet airplane that was both suitable for an attack role and capable of transporting heavy payloads of bombs over vast distances under any conditions. The answer was the Grumman A-6 Intruder. We thought of making a model that was a little friendlier. Without bombs and weapons it goes very far, and at the same time it is a model that you can have a lot of fun with.

The Grumman A-6 Intruder eats up distances. Easy to fold, yet an impressive design.

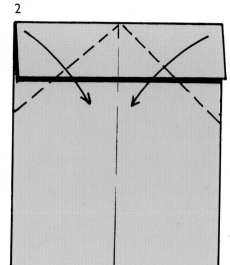

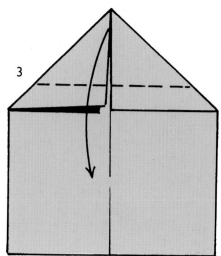

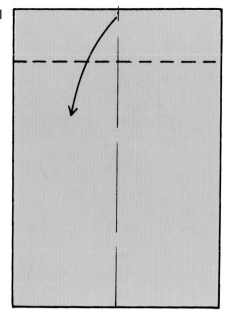

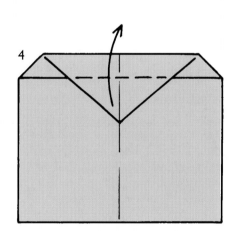

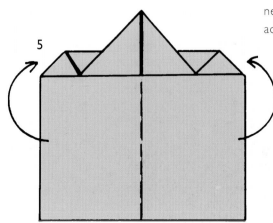

THE WINGS

1. Take an 8½ x 11 inch sheet of paper and fold the top edge downward.

2. Next, fold the corners to the inside to the middle of the sheet of paper.

3. Fold the points downward on the dotted line.

4. Then fold the point upward.

5. Finally, you fold the whole model in half to the back. The wings are nearly finished, except for the addition of the tail.

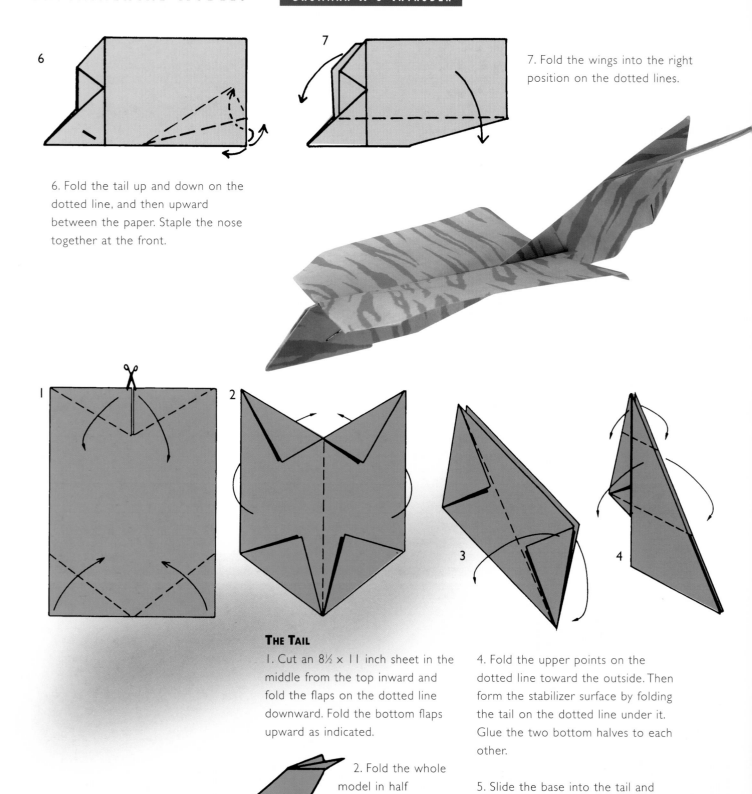

6

7. Fold the wings into the right position on the dotted lines.

6. Fold the tail up and down on the dotted line, and then upward between the paper. Staple the nose together at the front.

THE TAIL

1. Cut an 8½ x 11 inch sheet in the middle from the top inward and fold the flaps on the dotted line downward. Fold the bottom flaps upward as indicated.

2. Fold the whole model in half vertically.

3. Now fold both sides on the diagonal dotted line toward the outside.

4. Fold the upper points on the dotted line toward the outside. Then form the stabilizer surface by folding the tail on the dotted line under it. Glue the two bottom halves to each other.

5. Slide the base into the tail and glue. The Grumman A-6 is ready for its maiden flight.

In 1953 the Canadians made a serious effort to create a successor to the CF-100: the CF-105 Arrow. It was heralded for its supersonic speed and the vast distances it could cover. Unfortunately, due to the rise of effective unmanned missiles, the Canadian government decided in 1957 that they no longer needed the CF-105. The five that had already been built wound up on the scrap heap.

This will never happen to our paper model. Once you've flown it, you'll never want to get rid of it. It's not only a fast airplane, it's also extremely suitable for barrel rolls and loops.

What was that? It was the Avro Canada CF-105 soaring by, a superfast plane. For a better look at the model, turn the page.

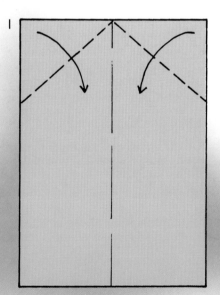

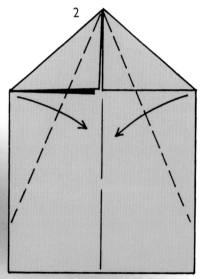

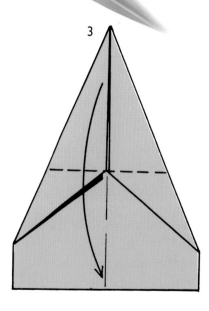

1. Take an 8½ x 11 inch sheet of paper, fold it in half lengthwise, and reopen it. Then fold the upper corners inward.

2. Fold the two sides on the dotted lines to the middle fold.

3. Then fold the tip downward against the bottom of the paper. Flatten the folds well.

The Avro Canada CF-105. In contrast to the paper model, the actual airplane was not a success.

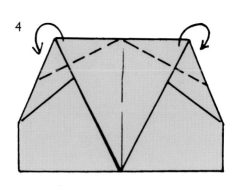

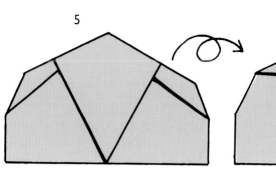

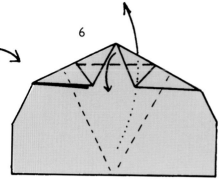

4. Fold the upper corners backward and double. Flatten the folds well.

5. and 6. Turn the model over and fold the tip that is now at the bottom upward on the dotted line. This you do by folding the short tip

downward. The larger tip under it now is on top.

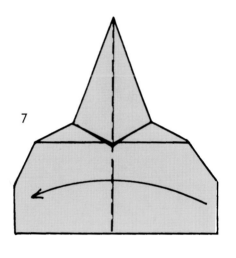

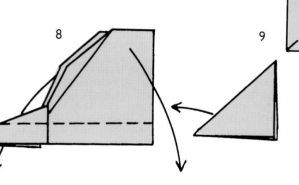

7. Fold the whole model in two. Again, remember to flatten the folds well, otherwise you'll end up with wrinkles in the wings, and this will have a negative influence on its flying ability.

8. Fold the wings horizontally on the dotted lines.

9. You make the stabilizer with a square, 4 x 4 inch square sheet of paper. Fold this in two on the diagonal dotted line and staple it to the tail. This stabilizer ensures a dead straight flight.

It could make you dizzy just by watching it, that's how fast the Chopper spins. Needless to say, the idea is to set it soaring from great heights. If you like, you can decrease the descent speed by folding the propeller blades horizontally. That way, the Chopper will take a longer time to get down, giving you the perfect opportunity to photograph it.

A simple strip of paper will suffice. And what could be nicer than to have ten of them turning around in the air at the same time?

1. Take a 10½ x 1 inch strip of paper. Fold it in the middle diagonally, into an L shape.

2. Make a second fold, from back to front, beside the first one so that the far ends are next to each other.

3. Fold the long piece fold again from back to front, once more creating an L shape that is square at the corner.

4. Fold the propellers on the dotted lines in the direction of the arrows. Then fold each

side of the square in the same direction.

5. Now fold the propellers at right angles to the rest. You can adjust the descent speed by changing this angle.

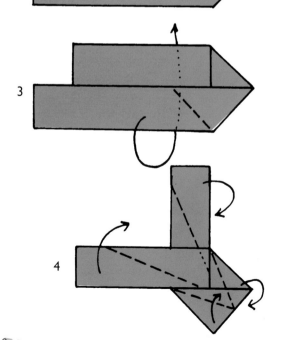

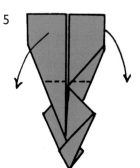

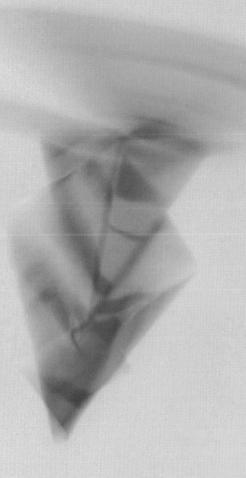

Descending straight down like a helicopter should. The descent speed can be adjusted. This model can be folded in just a few minutes.

STUNT FLYERS

Aviation acrobatics are sure to fire your imagination. Is there anyone who has never seen stunt flyers in action at least once, either live at an air show or on TV? All over the world teams of air acrobats perform the most spectacular stunts. These are of course well-trained and experienced pilots flying super truly high-quality planes. This is where the challenge for the paper plane pilot comes in. After all, what could be nicer than to fold one of those fantastic models out of a simple sheet of paper? Paper planes can perform stunts just as spectacular as those of real planes, and maybe even better. A loop is a piece of cake for a paper stunt flyer. And with great ease, it'll do a few extra rounds for you. All you need to do to achieve this is to turn the wing flaps up a little. If you fold one flap a little upward and the other a little downward, your plane will spin on its axis while it is flying—the barrel roll. An extreme form of the barrel roll is the corkscrew or victory roll.

The Saab Viggen 2004 boasts an enormous reach.

The tail, too, can be folded in a special way to make horizontal stunts possible. And the marvelous aspect of being the pilot of a paper flyer is that you can stay on the ground and just enjoy looking at all the beautiful stunts being performed in the air. If your plane does unexpectedly crash, well, you get going right away at constructing a new one, of course! By the way, keep in mind that a good air show absolutely needs some competition and people to watch it. Challenge your neighbors or colleagues into a stunt flying competition. Together, you will have lots of fun looking at all those paper capers, and you might even get to witness the crash of somebody else's plane. . .

WING-NOSE

This plane is one of the best stunt flyers ever, thanks to its double nose wing and adjustable wing rudder. To optimally enjoy the enormous reach of the Wing-Nose, fly it from a high starting point—a balcony, for example, or an attic window. This plane is extremely suitable for acrobatics, but it can also compete with the best when it comes to distance flight. In other words, better take something to eat and drink with you—this stunt flyer takes a very long time to get down to the ground!

THE WINGS

1. Take a 9½ x 1 inch strip of paper and fold it in the middle lengthwise, then fold each half again in the middle. Fold the two upper corners inward against the fold in the middle and then open them again.

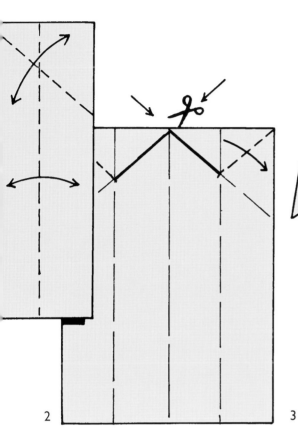

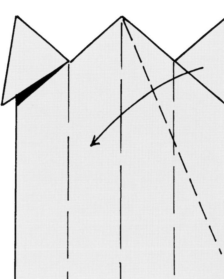

2

2. Take the scissors and cut into the top edge at the indicated spots (marked with a heavy line). Now fold the tips outward against the outside of the paper.

3

3. Fold the right side inward against the fold in the middle of the paper.

4

4. Fold the tip that is protruding over the middle toward the right on the dotted line.

Thanks to its large tail rudder and nose wings, the Wing-Nose has all the qualities needed for acrobatic performances.

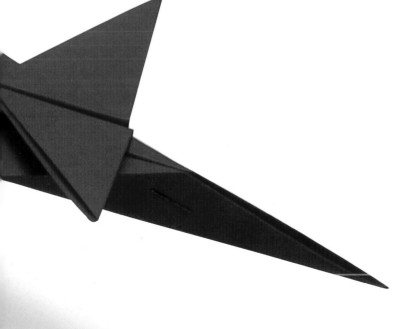

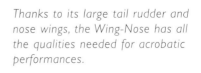

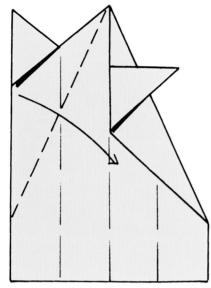

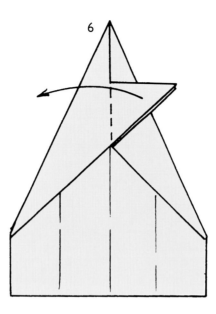

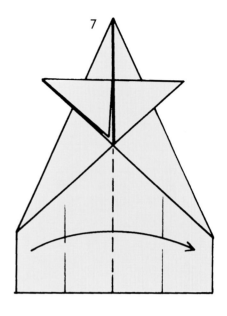

5. Make the same fold to the right so that the tip ends up exactly on the right half.

6. Fold the upper tip back to the left.

7. Fold the whole thing in two and flatten the folds well.

8. Fold the wings outward to both sides and create a stabilizer in the tail by folding back and forth on the diagonal line and then folding the tip upward between the paper.

9. Fold the two front wing tips outward on the dotted line.

THE TAIL RUDDER

1. Take a 4 x 6 inch strip of paper and fold one corner inward diagonally.

2. Cut the protruding part into the shape indicated in the drawing. Then make a sharp fold on the dotted line. Glue this tail part onto the stabilizer in the tail. It serves to determine the direction of the plane.

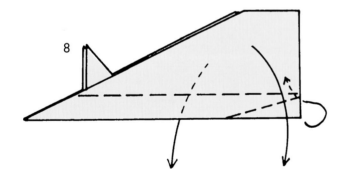

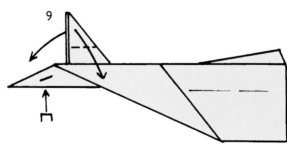

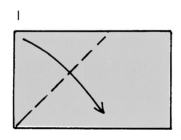

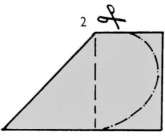

By folding the wing tips upward or downward the plane flies up or down. By folding the wing tips in opposite direction a barrel roll is created.

This is the same Wing-Nose but folded just a bit differently. The wings were folded from front to back diagonally upward, and there is no tail rudder. This makes the planes less easy to maneuver to the right or the left, but it still is an excellent plane for loops and barrel rolls.

Not only is the Eagle X-1 graceful and attractive, it can also be used for many different purposes. As a super-fast fighter, it enjoys great success at distance competitions. The Eagle also performs well as an acrobatic aircraft, partly because of its elegant shape. An extra dimension is added to the Eagle if you insert the wing folds so that the nose is weightier. The flight of the Eagle X-1 is just as majestic as that of its living namesake.

The Eagle X-1 has everything going for it and performs well in several areas.

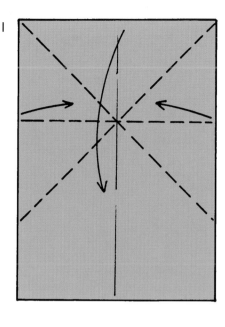

1. Take an 8½ x 11 inch sheet of paper. Fold it on the dotted lines back and forth. Flatten the folds well.

2. Fold the upper tips inward against the middle axis of the sheet of paper.

3. Fold the tip downward.

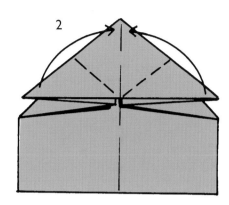

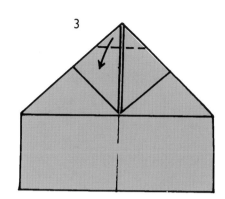

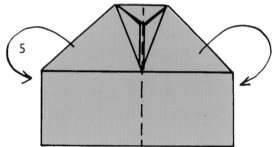

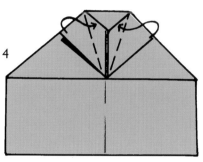

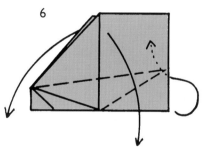

4. Fold the side tips of the nose inward and insert them into the sides of the tip you have folded downward before.

5. Fold the whole thing in two. The nose is thick and needs extra attention while folding it.

6. In the tail, make a fold on the dotted line. Then fold the tip inward and upward. The wings are folded out on the relevant dotted lines.

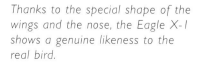

Thanks to the special shape of the wings and the nose, the Eagle X-1 shows a genuine likeness to the real bird.

In contrast to its big brother the bomber, our Avro Vulcan was especially designed for performance flights, as acrobatics are sometimes called. The characteristics of this model are the stabilizer on the nose, the large wing surface, and the stabilizer in the back. This plane can easily cover a distance of 5 to 10 yards (4.5–9 m) while at the same time doing a complete barrel roll or loop. The Avro Vulcan is easy to make and a joy to watch in flight, thanks to the minimalism of its design. The experienced folder will make two or three of them and let them fly in formation.

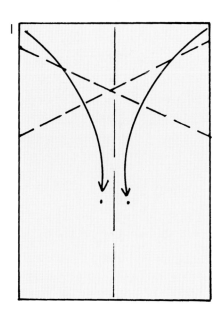

THE BODY

1. Take an 8½ x 11 inch sheet of paper and make a vertical fold exactly in the middle. Then fold the two upper corners down as shown.

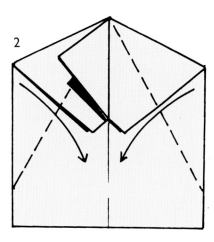

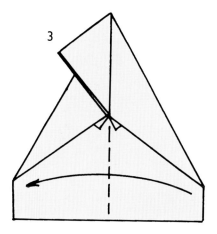

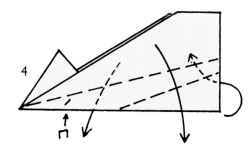

2. Flatten the folds well, creating a raised tip. Fold the side edges inward on the dotted lines against the fold in the center.

3. Fold the whole thing in two and flatten it well.

4. Make a stabilizer in the tail by folding back and forth on the dotted line and then folding the tip inward and upward.

5. Fold out the side edges on the dotted lines. The fuselage is ready.

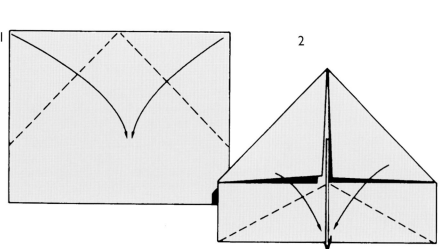

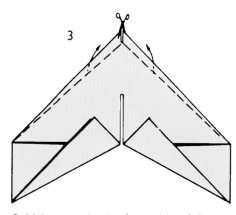

THE WING

1. Fold the upper corners of an 8½ x 11 inch sheet of paper inward so the tips touch each other in the middle.

2. Make cuts as indicated and fold the flaps upward on the dotted line.

3. Make a cut in the front side of the wing and then fold the edges slightly upward on the dotted lines. This is the bottom of the wing. It has to be turned over for the body to be attached.

THE ASSEMBLY

Slide the wing into the back stabilizer at the notch and glue together. The tip of the wing is now exactly lined up with nose. To provide the Avro Vulcan with even more stability, you can fold the wing tips upward.

The paper version of the Avro Vulcan held against the light. Like its big brother, the massive delta bomber, it possesses excellent aerodynamic qualities.

Origami specialist James M. Skoda was responsible for the idea of the nose of this aesthetic plane. Its origin is very clearly in the special Japanese art of origami. Together with the tail, which is at the base of all paper airplanes, it is a direct imitation of the Saab 37 Viggen.

Because it is such an advanced paper plane with great capacities, we baptized it the Saab Viggen 2004.

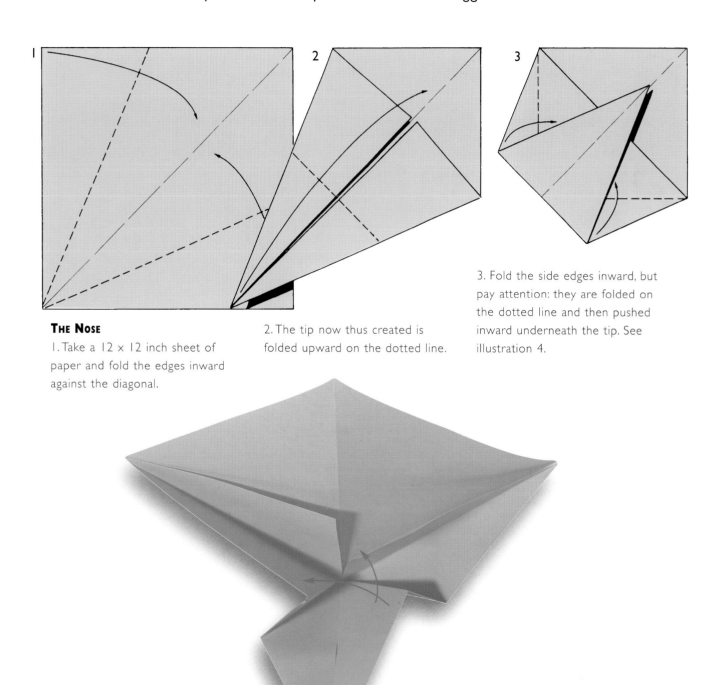

THE NOSE

1. Take a 12 x 12 inch sheet of paper and fold the edges inward against the diagonal.

2. The tip now thus created is folded upward on the dotted line.

3. Fold the side edges inward, but pay attention: they are folded on the dotted line and then pushed inward underneath the tip. See illustration 4.

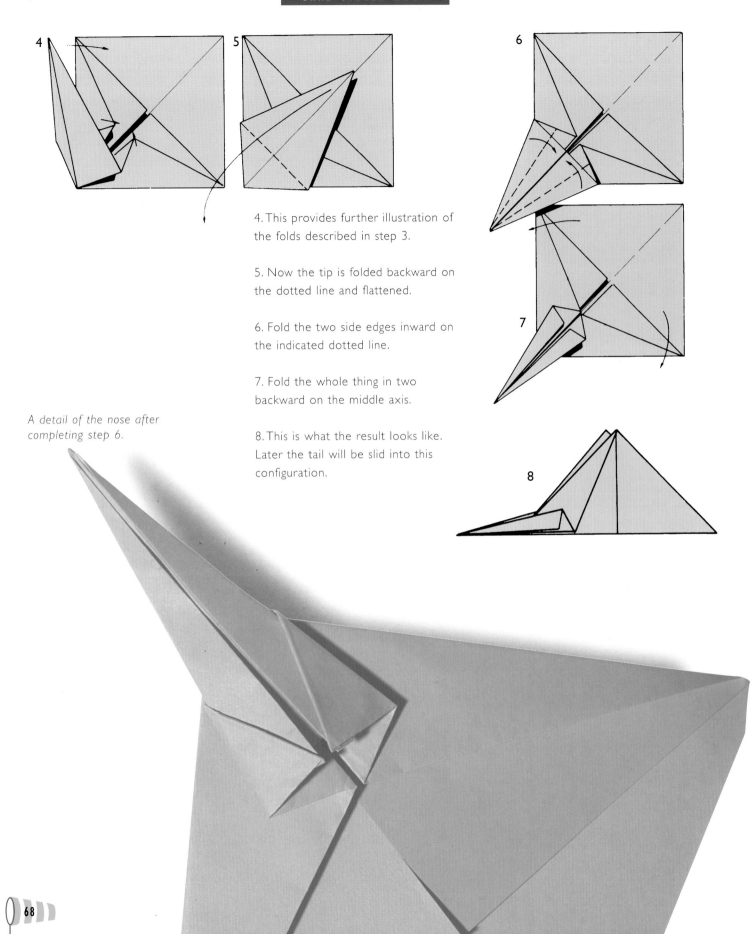

4. This provides further illustration of the folds described in step 3.

5. Now the tip is folded backward on the dotted line and flattened.

6. Fold the two side edges inward on the indicated dotted line.

7. Fold the whole thing in two backward on the middle axis.

8. This is what the result looks like. Later the tail will be slid into this configuration.

A detail of the nose after completing step 6.

1
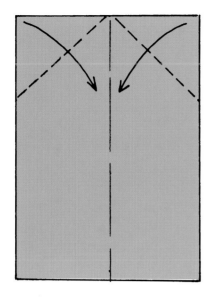

2
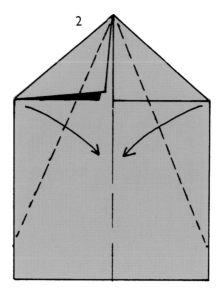

3
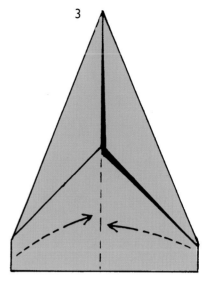

THE TAIL

1. Make a vertical fold in an 8½ x 11 inch sheet of paper. Then fold both the upper corners against this fold.

2. Fold the side edges of the paper inward on the dotted lines.

3. Now fold the whole thing in two. Flatten the folds well.

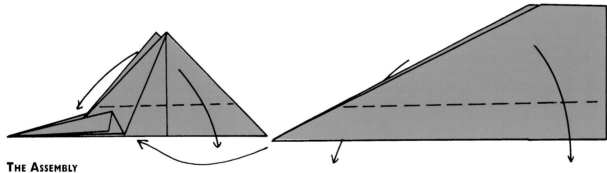

THE ASSEMBLY

Push the tip of the tail underneath the folds in the nose (see drawing). In the nose and tail fold the wings outward in the correct horizontal position. Staple the two parts together at the front of the nose.

A detail of the bottom of the plane, showing how the tail is slid into the nose.

A squadron of Saab Viggen 2004s in flight. Although easy to fold, the plane looks impressive.

The 1937 Japanese Nakajima was a reliable fighter that could achieve a speed of 285 mph (459 kph). A total of 3,384 were made, but none has survived. Our paper version is very fast indeed, eminently suitable for nose dives on targets. So maybe it does have a little kamikaze in its personality...

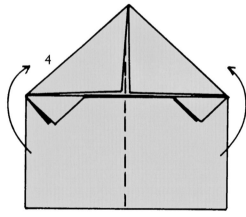

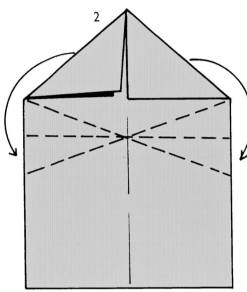

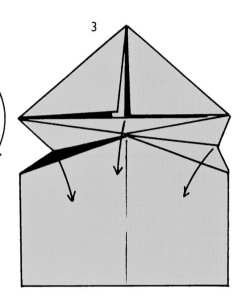

1. Make a vertical fold in the middle of an 8½ x 11 inch sheet of paper. Then fold the upper corners against this fold.

2. Fold the diagonal right top edge against the right side of the paper. This creates a fold on the dotted line. Do the same with the left side.

3. Make another horizontal fold through the intersection of the two diagonal folds and fold the whole thing forward like an accordion. Then fold the tip back and upward to produce the shape shown in illustration 4.

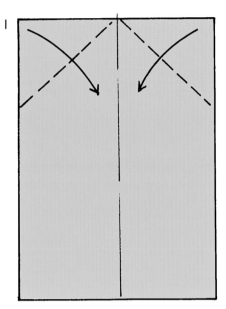

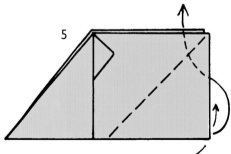

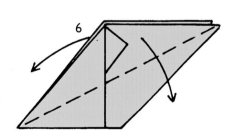

4. Flatten the folds well and fold the whole thing in two backward.

5. Fold back and forth on the dotted line and then push the tip upward via the inside.

6. On the dotted lines fold the wings to either sides. Staple the nose together.

*The Nakajima making a nose dive. A fine
plane for nose dives and barrel rolls.*

The Super Glider is a brilliant performer when it comes to loops, barrel rolls, and other forms of air acrobatics. In the world of paper planes it is unique. The wings are connected with an arrow-shaped, rolled-up piece of paper.

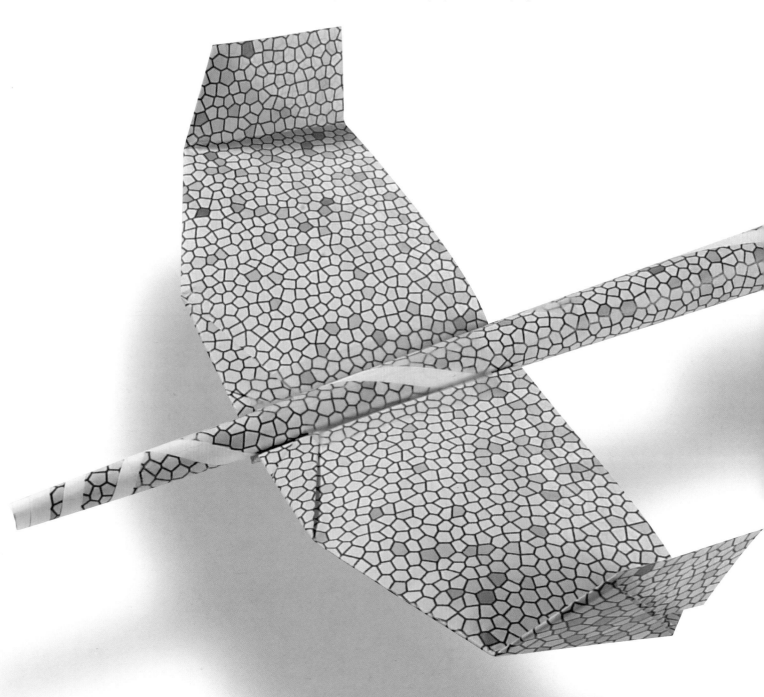

1

Tape the front wing to the body. To attach the front wing, make three cuts into the body and you slide the wing into these.

2

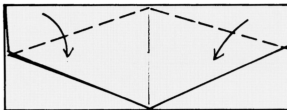

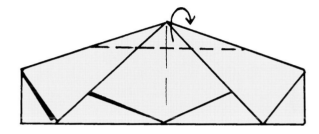

3

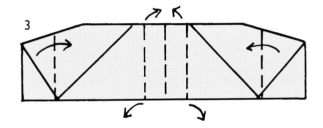

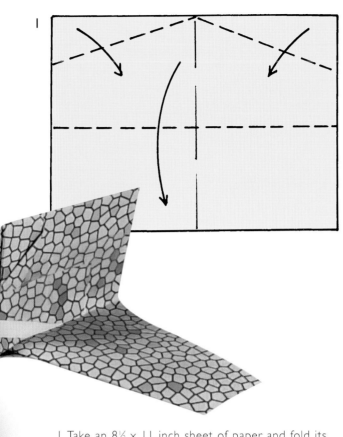

4

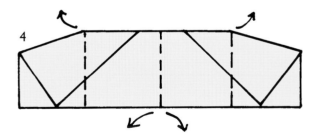

1. Take an 8½ x 11 inch sheet of paper and fold its upper corners inward. Then fold the sheet in two.

2. Again fold the corners inward and then the tip backward.

3. To make the big wing fold a V shape in the middle and the wing tips upward.

4. For the back wing you use an 8½ x 5½ inch sheet of paper. This you fold in the same way as the big wing.

Fold this wing in two and fold the tips outward.

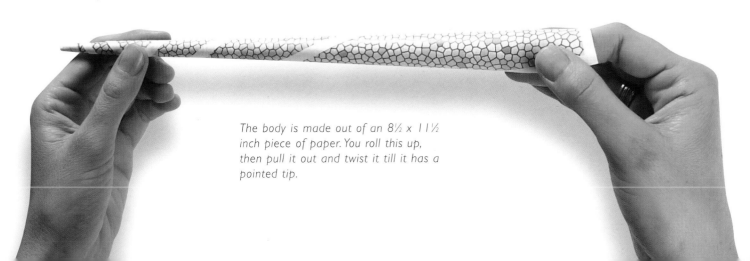

The body is made out of an 8½ x 11½ inch piece of paper. You roll this up, then pull it out and twist it till it has a pointed tip.

Dornier built various types of flying boats, but the model with the best aerodynamics was undoubtedly the Do-26. The Do-26 was developed for transporting mail across the Atlantic. Our paper model only takes one letter per flight. But you can combine it with a nice loop or corkscrew roll in the direction of the person addressed.

A one-letter flight, that is what our flying boat specializes in.

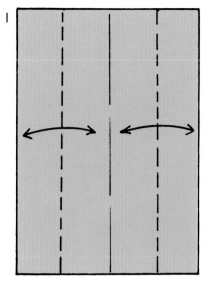

1. Fold an 8½ x 11 inch sheet of paper in half vertically. Open it up again and fold the side edges against the fold in the middle.

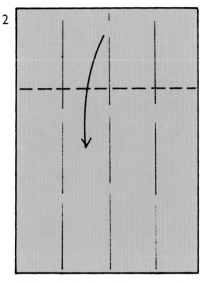

2. Turn back the sides so you have a flat sheet of paper again and then fold the upper part some 4½ inches downward.

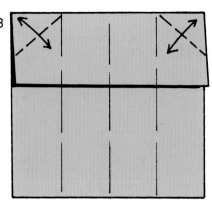

3. Make sharp folds inward on the dotted lines in both upper corners. Then turn them back to have a fleet sheet of paper again.

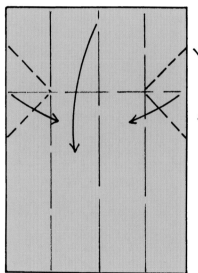

4. Fold the upper part downward and at the same time fold both sides inward in between the upper and lower part of the sheet. Flatten the folds well.

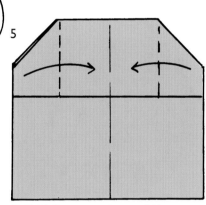

5. Fold the upper layer of the upper part inward.

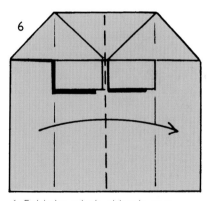

6. Fold the whole thing in two.

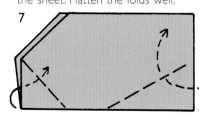

7. Fold back and forth in both corners on the dotted line and then fold both corners upward in between the paper.

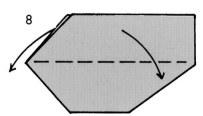

8. Fold the wings into a horizontal position. The nose is folded open a little for the flying. The back wing tips determine the flight.

Breakneck speed straight to its target—that's the dominant characteristic of the Arrow X-1. Folding it is a bit difficult, but the result makes it worthwhile. Thanks to its solid fuselage, it is a plane with a lot of mass, and thus it can achieve high speeds.

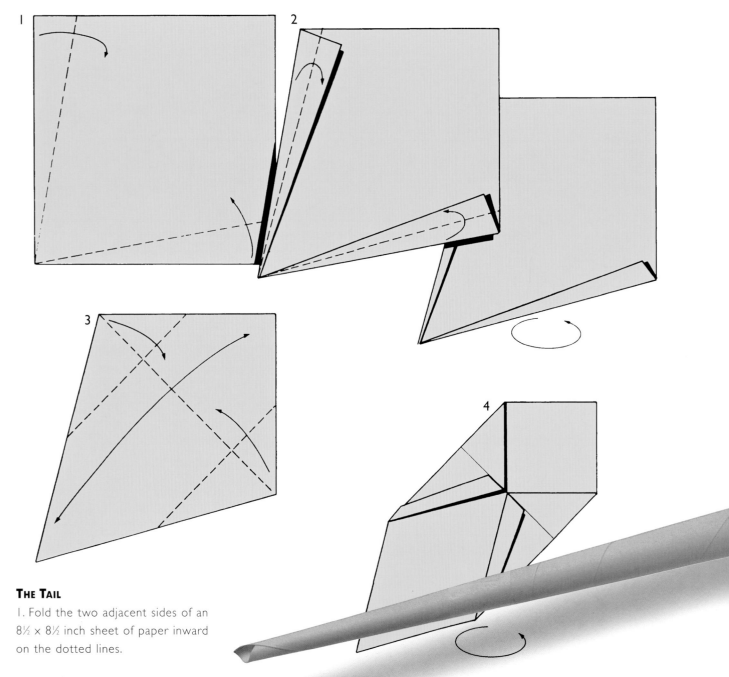

THE TAIL

1. Fold the two adjacent sides of an 8½ x 8½ inch sheet of paper inward on the dotted lines.

2. Repeat this as indicated in the drawing. Then turn the whole thing over.

3. Make a fold on the diagonal dotted line and fold back. Now fold the two sides inward.

4. This is what it looks like now. Turn it over again.

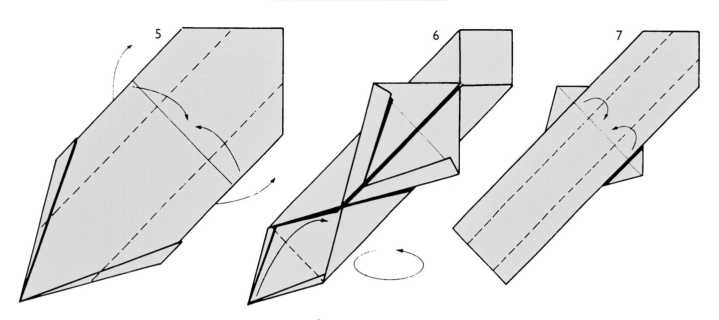

5. While you are folding the two sides inward you also take out the flaps underneath (see the arrows and illustration 6).

6. The point of the nose is folded upward and inward on the dotted line and the whole thing is turned over again.

7. Fold along the indicated lines and in the direction of the arrows. Then you fold these two strips of paper against each other. You are now ready to slide it into the body.

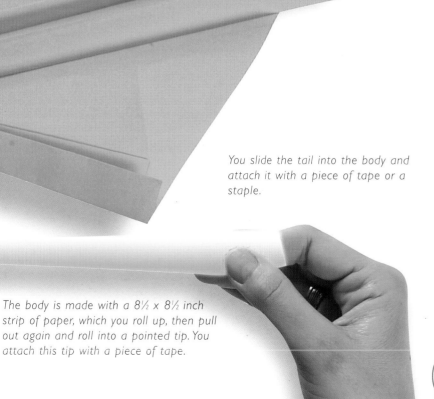

You slide the tail into the body and attach it with a piece of tape or a staple.

The body is made with a 8½ x 8½ inch strip of paper, which you roll up, then pull out again and roll into a pointed tip. You attach this tip with a piece of tape.

CREATIVE FLIGHTS

You have become acquainted with a great variety of paper planes in all possible shapes and sizes, each model with its own specific flying characteristics. Many different ways of folding have been introduced, and in the future we might even develop new ones. But making paper planes is also very well suited for something else—creating multiples, or planes consisting of various (parts of) other planes. It's a very creative and exciting activity, and these new models all boast the same impressive flying characteristics as the models they are derived from. Thinking up combinations of various planes offers endless possibilities—and you might make great discoveries!

For example, how about an Avro Vulcan with not one wing but three? Or a triple Eagle X-1? Or a Double-Wing Special with three nose parts and one wing? A whole new world will open up for you when you start being creative this way.

There is one principle you should always keep in mind: the center of gravity of the plane should be in its nose. If it is not, it will fall backwards and crash to the ground, or end up in an uncontrollable tailspin.

The model was created by combining the Fairey FD.2 and the Double-Wing Special, both of which are shown and described in this book.

A combination of the Simple Jet and the Avro Canada CF-105. Notice how different it looks, even though only minor changes were made.

The Arrow X-3 is a good example of a multiple. By sliding three Arrow X-1 tails into each other, this impressive plane benefits from excellent flying characteristics—it performs especially well over long distances.

THE ASSEMBLY

The Arrow X-3 is a triple Arrow X-1. Nose and tail are folded into each other and secured with a staple. It might be fun to try to make four or five planes into one. The fuselage is firm enough for it.

*The three tails are slid into each other
at the tip. When making the second
and third tails, ignore step 6.*

This multiple was made of the Fairey FD.2 on page 32, with the tail of the Double-Wing Special on page 28. Even though some minor changes were made to the tail, it is essentially the same—a fast airplane with impressive gliding possibilities. It will stay in the air for some 20 yards (18 m) or even more.

THE TAIL

The tail of the Double-Wing Special on page 28 is folded vertically instead of horizontally. The tail gets a V shape in its center, and this V shape is slid into the model of the Fairey FD.2 and stapled.

The result of combining the Fairey FD.2 and the Double-Wing Special, both shown and described in this book. Although its appearance is completely different, the excellent flying characteristics remain the same.

A super multiple, this Wing-Nose LDG is a combination
of the Wing-Nose on page 58 and the Long-Distance
Glider on page 9.
Two of the latter were slid into the model of the Wing-
Nose and secured with a staple. This results in enormous
lift. It takes quite a bit of folding, but the result more
than makes up of for it.

THE NOSE

Make the Wing-Nose as described on
page 58, but leave out the stabilizer in
the tail. Now slide the nose of the
Long-Distance Glider into it, which is
to function as the tail of the model.

THE TAIL

This consists of two Long-Distance
Gliders, but only one, the one in the
back, has a stabilizer. You can also
replace this stabilizer with the one
from the Avro Canada CF-105 on
page 51. Thanks to the size of this
stabilizer, the plane follows an
extremely steady course.

You can make the Wing-Nose LDG. as long as you like—a true custom made paper airplane.

Both planes are a combination of the Simple Jet and the Avro Canada CF-105. They look completely different even though only minor changes were made. The impressive flying capacities of the two planes are still intact.

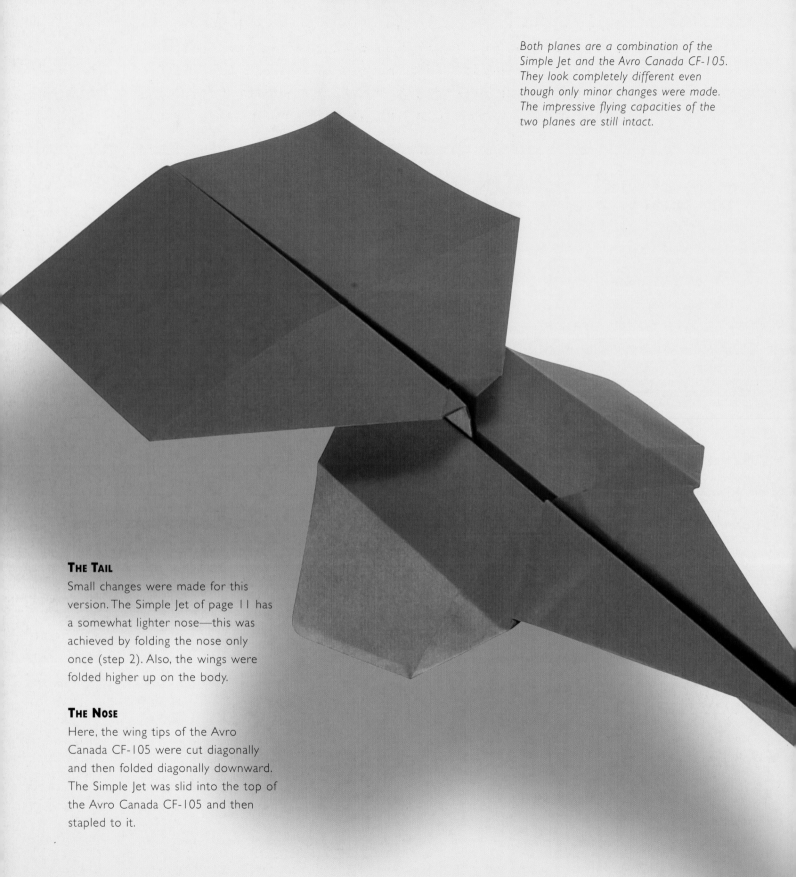

THE TAIL

Small changes were made for this version. The Simple Jet of page 11 has a somewhat lighter nose—this was achieved by folding the nose only once (step 2). Also, the wings were folded higher up on the body.

THE NOSE

Here, the wing tips of the Avro Canada CF-105 were cut diagonally and then folded diagonally downward. The Simple Jet was slid into the top of the Avro Canada CF-105 and then stapled to it.

Combining the Avro Canada CF-105 on page 51 with the Simple Jet on page 11 is a simple way to make nice variations with good flying capacities. Because both planes have a large wing surface and the Avro Canada CF-105 also possesses a firm, pointed nose, this combination has a vast reach.

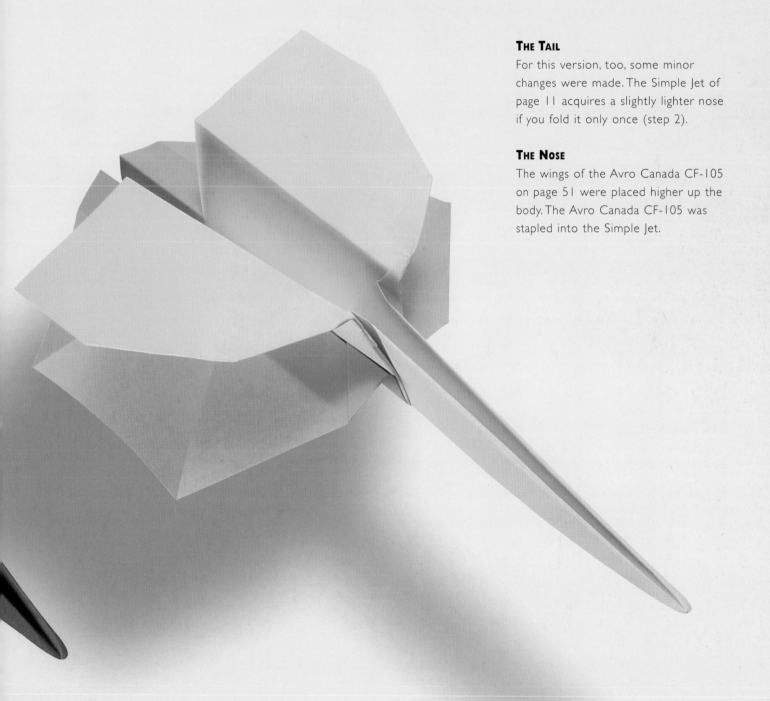

THE TAIL

For this version, too, some minor changes were made. The Simple Jet of page 11 acquires a slightly lighter nose if you fold it only once (step 2).

THE NOSE

The wings of the Avro Canada CF-105 on page 51 were placed higher up the body. The Avro Canada CF-105 was stapled into the Simple Jet.

Embroidering on the combination of the Avro Canada CF-105 of page 51 and the Simple Jet of page 11 (as shown on the previous pages), you'll get new ideas all the time. History played a role in developing this new model—Sir Francis Chichester's world-famous biplane, which he flew from England to Australia in the 1920s, had enormous influence in the design of it.
The Simple Jet was made several times, but each time the wings were placed in a higher spot. This resulted in a plane that flies astonishingly well. Here is a Super Tiger Moth from 2004.

THE TAIL

Small changes were made for this version. The Simple Jet of page 11 has a lighter nose, thanks to the fact it was folded only once (step 2). Also, the wings were folded higher up each time, and the Simple Jets and the Avro Canada CF-105 were stapled together.

THE NOSE

The wings of the Avro Canada CF-105 of page 51 were cut diagonally. The planes were stapled together.

You can go on and on making variations on the planes of pages 11 and 51. This Super Tiger Moth is an excellent example!

A bizarre combination of the Flying Cow on page 20 and the Avro Vulcan on page 64. Virtually nothing has been changed in either model; one has just been stapled onto the other. Thanks to the large wings of both models, this plane is eminently suitable for a show flight over a long distances. Not a stunt flyer, but an impressive glider.

THE TAIL
Nothing was changed about the Avro Vulcan. Its nose fin was simply slid into the Flying Cow and stapled to it.

THE NOSE
The tail rudder of the Flying Cow was folded forward and slid into the flap there. This is clearly visible in the illustration.

Two models that have been combined without either undergoing any changes and still produce a completely new model.

It is also possible to use several models of one and the same plane, as we did here with the Arrowhead of page 16. The tail consists of a partially folded Arrowhead and is stapled into a complete Arrowhead.

A paper airplane consisting of several replicas of itself.

THE TAIL

The tail was folded according to steps 1 and 2, folded in two, and provided with the tail rudder of the original Arrowhead. Afterward the tail was slid into the nose and stapled together. The wings of the tail and nose were both folded into the right position.

THE NOSE

The tail rudder of the lower Arrowhead was not folded. The tail was slid into it and stapled to it.

All things must come to an end, and that includes paper
planes. Even though they differ in many ways—one is an air
acrobat and another a long-distance flyer, one quite complex
and the another very simple, and so on—unfortunately one
thing they all have in common is that their life spans are
short if they are flown intensively. Don't forget, however,
that a creative airplane builder, once he or she has become
enthusiastic about the results, will continue to develop
new models, and at an ever increasing speed. Ah, well,
then there's just the problem of where to leave the
old ones...

INDEX

METRIC EQUIVALENCY CHART

Inches to Centimeters

INCHES	CM
0.25	0.6
0.5	1.3
0.75	1.9
1	2.5
2	5.1
3	7.6
4	10.2
5	12.7
5.5	14.0
6	15.2
7	17.8
8	20.3
8.5	21.6
9	22.9
9.5	24.1
10	25.4
10.5	26.7
11	27.9
11.5	29.2
12	30.5

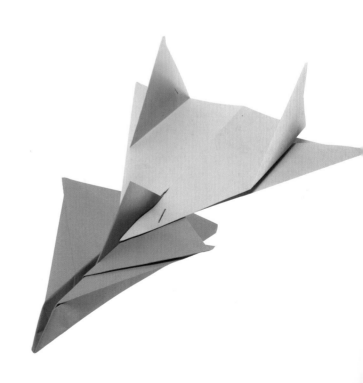